EDITOR: Maryanne Blacker

FOOD EDITOR: Pamela Clark

■ ■ ■

ART DIRECTOR: Rowena Sheppard

ARTIST: Mike Davey

PHOTOGRAPHER: Russell Brooks

■ ■ ■

TEST KITCHEN STAFF:

DEPUTY FOOD EDITOR: Jan Castorina

ASSISTANT FOOD EDITOR: Kathy Snowball

ASSOCIATE FOOD EDITOR:
Enid Morrison

SENIOR HOME ECONOMISTS: Alexandra McCowan,
Louise Patniotis, Kathy Wharton

HOME ECONOMISTS: Cynthia Black, Leisel Chen,
Tracey Kern, Jill Lange, Kathy McGarry,
Maggie Quickenden, Dimitra Stais

EDITORIAL COORDINATOR: Elizabeth Hooper

KITCHEN ASSISTANT: Amy Wong

■ ■ ■

HOME LIBRARY STAFF:

ASSISTANT EDITOR: Beverley Hudec

DESIGNERS: Paula Wooller, Robbylee Phelan

EDITORIAL COORDINATOR: Lara Quinlin

■ ■ ■

ACP PUBLISHER: Richard Walsh

ACP ASSOCIATE PUBLISHER: Bob Neil

■ ■ ■

Produced by The Australian Women's Weekly Home Library.
Typeset by Photoset Computer Service Pty Ltd, and Letter
Perfect, Sydney. Printed by Dai Nippon Co Ltd in Japan.
Published by Australian Consolidated Press,
54 Park Street Sydney.
♦ AUSTRALIA: Distributed by Network Distribution Company,
54 Park St Sydney (02) 282 8777.
♦ UNITED KINGDOM: Distributed in the U.K. by Australian
Consolidated Press (UK) Ltd, 20 Galowhill Rd, Brackmills,
Northampton NN4 OEE (0604) 760 456.
♦ CANADA: Distributed in Canada by Whitecap Books Ltd,
1086 West 3rd St, North Vancouver V7P 3J6 (604) 9809852.
♦ NEW ZEALAND: Distributed in New Zealand by Netlink
Distribution Company 17B Hargreaves St, Level 5,
College Hill, Auckland 1 (9) 302 7616.
♦ SOUTH AFRICA: Distributed in South Africa by Intermag,
PO Box 57394, Springfiled 2137 (011) 4933200.

■ ■ ■

Dinner Party Cookbook

Includes index.
ISBN 0 949892 68 8.

1. Cookery. 2. Entertaining. (Series :
Australian Women's Weekly Home
Library).

641.5'68

■ ■ ■

■ ■ ■

COVER: Souffle Oysters, Camembert Chicken and New
Potatoes, Green Salad with Avocado Dressing, Strawberry
Hazelnut Slice, page 98.
OPPOSITE: Broccoli with Seafood, page 118.

Dinner Party Cookbook

D0128718

Our amazing variety of menus will help you to plan confidently for success, whatever the occasion. The menus are in many styles, and mostly serve 4 to 6 people. There is also a smorgasbord and a champagne breakfast or brunch if you need to cater for more. The international menus make parties with a difference (the Scottish dinner would kick off the new year in style!). We also suggest ideas for people in a hurry, for those who don't eat meat, for slimmers and many more. The desserts and after-dinner treats are irresistible, too (slimmers turn those yummy pages quickly)! Our popular, do-ahead tips and step-by-step pictures help make much of the preparation easy.

Pamela Clark

FOOD EDITOR

BRITISH & NORTH AMERICAN READERS: Please note that Australian cup and spoon measurements are metric. Conversion charts for cup and spoon measurements and oven temperatures appear on page 128.

Avocado with Seafood
Steaks with Whisky Cream Sauce
Potato Casserole
Baked Zucchini
Mimosa Salad
Rockmelon Ice-cream

If you're celebrating an anniversary, or birthday, or just planning a special intimate dinner, this menu provides simple, delicious food. The potato casserole can be prepared the day before, all ready for final reheating; the dessert, too, can be prepared a day or two ahead. The balance of the menu comes together with a minimum of effort. The menu serves 2 but, of course, if you want to serve four people, the quantities are easy to double. The Rockmelon Ice-cream recipe serves 4

Opposite, clockwise from left: Avocado with Seafood, Mimosa Salad, Potato Casserole, Rockmelon Ice-cream, Steaks with Whisky Cream Sauce and Baked Zucchini.

AVOCADO WITH SEAFOOD
1 ripe avocado
lemon juice
125g (4oz) small prawns
SAUCE
¼ cup mayonnaise
3 teaspoons tomato sauce
1 teaspoon brandy
few drops tabasco
pinch curry powder
1 teaspoon lemon juice
2 shallots

Cut avocado in half lengthwise, remove stone. Brush cut surface of each half with lemon juice. Shell prawns, remove dark veins. Arrange prawns in each avocado half, spoon sauce over.

Sauce: Combine mayonnaise, tomato sauce, brandy, tabasco, curry powder, lemon juice and the chopped shallots; mix well.

Note: If desired, fresh or canned crab can be added to the prawns. ▷

STEAKS WITH WHISKY CREAM SAUCE

2 fillet steaks, about 2.5cm (1in.) thick
2 slices bread, about 2.5cm (1in.) thick
30g (1oz) butter
1 teaspoon french mustard
60g (2oz) butter, extra
1 teaspoon flour
1 shallot
3 tablespoons water
¼ cup cream
2 teaspoons chopped parsley
1 beef stock cube
1 tablespoon whisky
1 teaspoon lemon juice

Press steaks to a neat shape; cut bread into rounds about the same size as steaks. Heat butter in pan, add mustard, mix well. Brush bread on both sides with this mustard butter, place on oven tray, bake in moderate oven 20 minutes or until golden brown.

Heat extra butter in pan, add steaks, cook until done as desired. Remove from pan, keep warm. Drain off pan drippings, leaving 1 tablespoon in pan. Add flour, add finely-chopped shallot, stir over medium heat a few seconds. Stir in water, stir until sauce boils, add cream, parsley, crumbled stock cube, whisky and lemon juice, reduce heat, simmer 2 minutes.

POTATO CASSEROLE

250g (8oz) potatoes
15g (½oz) butter
1 egg
½ cup cream
60g (2oz) cheddar cheese
salt, pepper

Peel potatoes; cut in half, if large; cook in boiling salted water 15 to 20 minutes or until tender. Drain. Add butter and potatoes to pan, mash potatoes. Spread potatoes evenly over base of greased small ovenproof dish. Beat egg well, add cream and grated cheese, season with salt and pepper, pour over potato in dish. Bake uncovered in moderate oven approximately 30 minutes or until topping is set and golden.

MIMOSA SALAD

1 small lettuce
2 sticks celery
2 tomatoes
2 hard-boiled eggs
¼ cup french dressing
1 tablespoon cream

Wash and shred lettuce; slice celery diagonally; cut tomatoes into quarters, remove seeds, slice tomatoes thinly. Shell eggs, cut in halves, remove yolks; push egg yolks through sieve; cut egg whites into thin strips. Combine in bowl lettuce, celery, tomatoes, egg white strips and combined french dressing and cream, toss well. Sprinkle sieved egg yolk over the top.

BAKED ZUCCHINI

60g (2oz) butter
4 zucchinis

Put butter in small baking dish, stand over medium heat until melted, add halved zucchinis, bake in moderate oven 15 to 20 minutes or until golden.

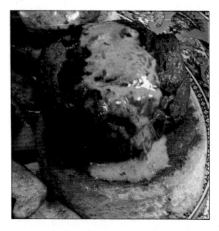

1 teaspoon gelatine
1 tablespoon water
2 egg yolks
¼ cup sugar
2 tablespoons orange juice
⅓ cup milk
300ml carton thickened cream
½ small ripe rockmelon
2 passionfruit

STEP 1

Sprinkle gelatine over water, dissolve over hot water. Beat egg yolks, sugar and orange juice until pale and fluffy. Put in top of double saucepan with milk, stir over simmering water until the mixture thickens slightly.

STEP 2

Remove from heat, add dissolved gelatine, beat until mixture is luke-warm, add cream, mix well. Pour mixture into freezer tray, freeze until it is firm.

STEP 3

Peel rockmelon, remove seeds, chop roughly, put into blender; blend until pureed. Measure rockmelon puree; use only 1 cup of the puree; water content in rockmelon is high and any extra puree will give an icy texture to the ice-cream. Spoon ice-cream into small bowl of electric mixer, beat until smooth and thick. Fold rockmelon puree and passionfruit pulp into ice-cream, pour into freezer tray, freeze until firm. If desired, top each serving with extra whipped cream and extra passionfruit pulp. ☐

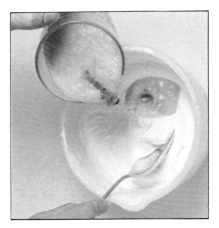

Vermouth Scallops
Beef in Red Wine
New Potatoes, Buttered Squash
Braised Leek Salad
Cheese Platter
Grand Marnier Mousse

This easy-to-prepare special menu for two presents French food at its best. Each course is simple, but superbly flavoured. And, if you're having friends to dinner, simply double the ingredients to serve 4

Opposite, clockwise from top left: Grand Marnier Mousse, Cheese Platter, Vermouth Scallops, Beef in Red Wine, Braised Leek Salad, New Potatoes and Buttered Squash

VERMOUTH SCALLOPS

8 scallops
¼ cup dry vermouth
1 tablespoon chopped parsley
1 teaspoon lemon juice
½ teaspoon sugar
salt, pepper
flour
1 egg
packaged dry breadcrumbs
60g (2oz) butter
1 tablespoon oil
1 tablespoon cream

Clean scallops. In a bowl combine vermouth, parsley, lemon juice, sugar, salt and pepper. Add scallops, marinade 2 hours. Drain scallops, reserve marinade. Coat scallops lightly with flour, dip in beaten egg, coat well with breadcrumbs. Thread four scallops on to each of two bamboo skewers. Heat butter and oil in pan, add scallops, cook until golden brown on both sides, 2 to 3 minutes. Remove from pan, drain, reserve 1 tablespoon pan drippings in pan. Add reserved marinade to pan, bring to boil, reduce heat, simmer uncovered 2 minutes, add cream, reheat without boiling. Put scallops on bed of hot rice with chopped parsley folded through (you will need to cook ¼ cup long grain rice). Spoon sauce over scallops. ▷

BEEF IN RED WINE

2 pieces fillet steak (see below)
75g (2½oz) butter
4 small onions
2 tablespoons flour
1¼ cups water
2 tablespoons red wine
1 tablespoon brandy
1 beef stock cube
1 tablespoon tomato paste
1 teaspoon french mustard
125g (4oz) small mushrooms

Remove any fat from meat, pound steaks out to 1cm (½in.) thickness. Melt butter in shallow pan, add steaks, cook until done as desired. Remove meat from pan, add peeled whole onions, cook few minutes, remove from pan. Stir in flour, cook 1 minute. Gradually stir in water and wine, add brandy, crumbled stock cube, tomato paste and mustard, mix well. Place steaks in small ovenproof dish, add onions and mushrooms, pour prepared sauce over, cover, bake in moderate oven 15 to 20 minutes.

Note: If steaks are small, you may need 4 steaks instead of the 2 specified.

BUTTERED SQUASH

6 squash
45g (1½oz) butter

Wash squash, place in pan, cook in boiling salted water 15 to 20 minutes or until squash are just tender. Drain, toss squash in butter over low heat until butter has melted.

BRAISED LEEK SALAD

2 small thin leeks
15g (½oz) butter
1 chicken stock cube
⅓ cup water
2 lettuce leaves

Trim leeks, leaving 8cm (3in.) of green part. Peel off outside layer, then make 2 cuts about 5cm (2in.) long, first one way then the other, on top of green parts of leeks. This makes it easy to ruffle back the tops when washing. Wash well to remove grit. Cut leeks in half lengthways. Melt butter in pan, add leeks, cook 2 minutes, add crumbled stock cube and water. Bring to boil, reduce heat, simmer covered 30 minutes or until tender; cool, then drain. Serve on bed of lettuce with the dressing spooned over.

DRESSING

¼ cup bottled french dressing
1 tablespoon chopped parsley

Combine dressing and parsley, mix until well combined.

CHEESE PLATTER

It is the French custom to serve the cheese before the dessert, accompanied by a glass of good red wine. We've chosen a camembert cheese (serve it at room temperature) with a beautiful pear, some slices of red apple and a few water biscuits on the cheese board.

GRAND MARNIER MOUSSE

2 oranges
3 tablespoons Grand Marnier
2 tablespoons sugar
2 eggs
1 teaspoon grated orange rind
1½ teaspoons gelatine
2 tablespoons orange juice
⅔ cup cream

Peel oranges, removing all white pith; cut oranges into segments; reserve two segments for decoration, roughly chop remaining orange segments. Pour one tablespoon Grand Marnier over, cover, leave for 30 minutes.

Place sugar and eggs in top of double saucepan. Beat over simmering water until mixture is thick and comes to top of pan. Remove pan from heat, stir in remaining Grand Marnier and grated orange rind. Sprinkle gelatine over orange juice, stand over hot water until gelatine has dissolved. Add dissolved gelatine mixture to egg mixture. Stand pan in cold water until mixture is cool, stirring occasionally. Beat cream until soft peaks form, fold into cooled orange mixture. Spoon marinated orange pieces into two serving dishes, pour mousse evenly over top of oranges. Refrigerate until set. Just before serving, top each with reserved orange segment.

60g (2oz) blanched almonds
2 tablespoons liquid glucose
60g (2oz) butter
¼ cup brown sugar, firmly packed
⅓ cup plain flour

STEP 1

Finely chop almonds. Combine glucose, butter and sugar in saucepan, stir over low heat until sugar is dissolved and butter melted. Increase heat, bring to boil, quickly remove from heat, immediately stir in sifted flour and almonds, mix well.

STEP 2

Lightly grease oven trays; too much greasing will cause biscuits to burn. Drop level teaspoonfuls of mixture on to trays, about 8cm (3in.) apart; biscuits will spread up to 10cm (4in.) in diameter. Bake up to 5 biscuits at a time, for easier handling. As shown, mixture will become firm as it cools, this does not affect the finished biscuit.

STEP 3

Bake in moderate oven 5 to 7 minutes, or until golden brown. Stand about a minute, or until edges of biscuits are firm enough to be loosened with spatula (do not let biscuits cool on trays, as they may be difficult to remove from trays when cold). Working quickly, carefully lift soft biscuits on to wire rack; biscuits become crisp on cooling. Store biscuits in airtight container. Makes about 25 biscuits. □

Smoked Trout Pate
Steaks with Brandy Cream Sauce
Vegetable Platter
Minted Cucumber Salad
Cherry Rum Cake

Here is a full-of-flavour dinner party menu. Both first course and dessert can be prepared the day before, leaving only the main course for attention on the day of the party. There's a colourful vegetable platter from which guests help themselves. The menu serves 4 people

Opposite, clockwise from top: Minted Cucumber Salad, Smoked Trout Pate, Steaks with Brandy Cream Sauce and Vegetable Platter, and Cherry Rum Cake.

SMOKED TROUT PATE
1 whole smoked trout, about 250g (8oz)
1 cup water
½ cup dry white wine
125g (4oz) butter
2 teaspoons gelatine
300ml carton sour cream
salt, pepper
1 small ripe avocado
lemon juice

Carefully remove skin and bones from trout. Place skin and head of trout into pan, add water and wine. Bring to boil, reduce heat, simmer covered for 5 minutes. Strain through fine sieve. Return liquid to pan, add butter and gelatine, stir over low heat until butter has melted and gelatine dissolved. Place liquid into blender, add trout meat. Blend on medium speed for 2 minutes or until finely pureed. Pour into bowl, leave until cold. Fold in sour cream, season with salt and pepper. Pour into 4 individual serving dishes. Cover and refrigerate overnight. Just before serving, remove skin and seed from avocado, cut into thin slices, toss lightly in lemon juice, arrange on top of trout plate. Serve with small toast triangles.   ▷

STEAKS WITH BRANDY CREAM SAUCE

125g (4oz) butter
4 fillet steaks
1 clove garlic
2 teaspoons french mustard
2 tablespoons brandy
2 tablespoons water
salt, pepper
3 tablespoons cream

Heat 60g (2oz) of the butter in frying pan, add steaks, cook until done as desired. Remove from pan, keep warm. Add remaining 60g (2oz) butter to pan, stir until melted. Add crushed garlic, saute 1 minute, add mustard, stir until smooth. Add brandy, water, salt and pepper, stir until sauce boils, add cream, reduce heat, simmer 1 minute. Serve steaks with sauce spooned over.

VEGETABLE PLATTER

Asparagus: Open 470g can asparagus spears, put asparagus and liquid in saucepan, simmer covered 2 minutes, drain.

Mushrooms: Saute 185g (6oz) mushrooms in 60g (2oz) melted butter until lightly browned.

Carrots: Peel 3 large carrots, cut into 5cm (2in.) strips. Drop in boiling salted water, boil covered 3 minutes, drain.

Potatoes: Peel 4 medium potatoes. Cut in half, cook in boiling salted water 3 minutes. Drain and allow to become cold. Deep-fry in hot oil until they are golden brown and cooked through.

Artichokes: Open 400g can artichokes, put in saucepan with liquid, simmer covered 1 minute, drain and serve topped with prepared Buttered Lemon Sauce.

BUTTERED LEMON SAUCE

2 egg yolks
1 tablespoon lemon juice
90g (3oz) butter
salt, pepper

Place egg yolks, lemon juice and roughly-chopped softened butter in top of double saucepan, stir over barely simmering water until butter has melted and mixture is thick. Remove from water immediately. Season with salt and pepper.

MINTED CUCUMBER SALAD

1 small lettuce
1 small cucumber
MINT DRESSING
3 tablespoons chopped mint
2 tablespoons oil
2 tablespoons white vinegar
salt, pepper
½ teaspoon sugar
pinch dry mustard

Wash and dry lettuce. Cut cucumber into very thin slices. Place lettuce and cucumber into bowl, refrigerate until ready to serve. To serve, tear lettuce into medium-sized pieces. Place lettuce, cucumber and prepared Mint Dressing into bowl; toss lightly.

Mint Dressing: Put all ingredients into screw-top jar, shake well. Shake the dressing again just before using.

CHOCOLATE SPONGE

¼ cup plain flour
¼ cup self-raising flour
¼ teaspoon salt
60g (2oz) dark chocolate
4 eggs
½ cup castor sugar
1 teaspoon vanilla
¼ teaspoon bicarbonate of soda
2 tablespoons water
castor sugar, extra

FILLING

470g can black cherries
1 teaspoon vanilla
2 tablespoons sugar
2 tablespoons rum
300ml carton thickened cream

TOPPING

½ cup thickened cream
¼ teaspoon vanilla
30g (1oz) dark chocolate

Filling: Drain and pit cherries. Place vanilla, sugar, rum and cream into bowl, beat cream until firm peaks form.

Topping: Place cream and vanilla into bowl, beat until firm peaks form. Place chopped chocolate in top of double saucepan over simmering water, stir until chocolate has melted.

STEP 1

Sift together flours and salt. Melt roughly-chopped chocolate in top of double saucepan over simmering water. Beat eggs, sugar and vanilla together until thick and creamy, making sure all sugar is dissolved. Fold in sifted flour mixture. Add combined bicarbonate of soda and water to chocolate, stir until smooth; fold quickly and evenly into egg-and-flour mixture.

STEP 2

Pour into greased and greased-paper-lined 30cm x 25cm (12in. x 10in.) swiss roll tin. Bake in moderately hot oven 12 to 15 minutes or until roll springs back when centre is pressed. Turn out immediately on to tea towel lightly dusted with castor sugar. Peel off paper, trim edges with sharp knife.

STEP 3

Roll cake up in tea towel like a swiss roll. Allow to become cold.

STEP 4

Unroll cake. Place the well-drained, pitted cherries side by side along the short edge at one side of the cake. Spread the rum cream over the whole cake and roll it up again, starting from the end which has the cherries, so they are in the middle of the cake. Cover cake with plastic food wrap and refrigerate several hours or overnight.

For the **topping,** spoon whipped cream into piping bag fitted with star nozzle. Pipe cream decoratively in swirls on top of cake. Spoon melted chocolate into one corner of small plastic bag. Cut the tip off corner, and drizzle chocolate over cream. Refrigerate cake until serving time. ☐

Smoked Roe Pate
Asparagus Chicken with
Parsley Butter
Potato Casserole
Mushroom Salad
Strawberry Chocolate Box

A light, full-of-flavour dinner party for 4 — perfect for summer weather. And there's a superb dessert which we've created especially for this dinner party. It's a box made of chocolate, filled with a brandied chocolate cream and topped with glazed strawberries; it cuts perfectly into four individual servings

Opposite, clockwise from left: Smoked Roe Pate, Strawberry Chocolate Box, Mushroom Salad, Potato Casserole, and Asparagus Chicken with Parsley Butter.

SMOKED ROE PATE
250g (8oz) smoked roe
250g (8oz) packaged cream cheese
300ml carton sour cream
2 tablespoons chopped parsley
2 gherkins
salt, pepper
1 tablespoon lemon juice
1 teaspoon french mustard

Carefully remove thin skin from roe. Put cream cheese into bowl; beat until soft and creamy. Add roughly-chopped roe; beat until well combined. Add sour cream, parsley, finely-chopped gherkins, salt, pepper, lemon juice and mustard; mix well. Spoon into serving bowl; cover, refrigerate overnight. ▷

ASPARAGUS CHICKEN

4 chicken breasts
2 rashers bacon
1 small onion
15g (½oz) butter
½ x 310g can asparagus cuts
salt, pepper
flour
1 egg
2 tablespoons milk
packaged dry breadcrumbs
60g (2oz) butter, extra
2 tablespoons oil
PARSLEY BUTTER
125g (4oz) butter
1 tablespoon chopped parsley
1 tablespoon chopped shallots
salt, pepper

Remove skin from chicken breasts. Carefully remove chicken meat from bones, giving 8 individual pieces, gently and lightly pound each chicken breast. Chop bacon finely; peel onion, chop finely. Saute onion and bacon in butter until onion is transparent, add drained and finely-chopped asparagus, salt and pepper, remove from heat, cool. Cut a pocket in each chicken breast, fill with asparagus mixture. Coat chicken breasts lightly with flour, dip in combined beaten egg and milk, coat well with breadcrumbs. Heat extra butter and oil in large frying pan, add chicken, cook until golden brown on each side and cooked through; allow approximately 3 minutes cooking time on each side. Serve immediately with Parsley Butter.

Parsley Butter: Beat butter until smooth and creamy, add parsley, shallots, salt and pepper, beat well. Spoon mixture in a rough log shape about a quarter of the way down a sheet of greaseproof paper. Fold paper over roll, then with ruler push against the butter so that the mixture forms a smooth roll. Roll in the greaseproof paper, refrigerate until firm. Cut into slices.

POTATO CASSEROLE

1kg (2lb) potatoes
salt, pepper
½ cup milk
300ml carton cream
1 clove garlic
4 shallots
30g (1oz) butter

Peel potatoes, cut into thin slices; pat dry with tea towel; add salt and pepper, toss lightly. Put milk and potatoes into saucepan; bring to boil, reduce heat, simmer gently covered 10 minutes. Add cream and crushed garlic, simmer covered further 20 minutes. Add shallots. Spoon potatoes and liquid into casserole. Dot with butter; bake uncovered in a moderate oven 10 minutes or till golden brown.

MUSHROOM SALAD

250g (8oz) mushrooms
1 red pepper
1 green pepper
4 shallots
1 tablespoon chopped parsley
¼ cup french dressing
salt, pepper

Slice mushrooms; seed red and green peppers, chop finely; chop shallots. Combine parsley, french dressing, salt and pepper; mix well. Add to vegetables, toss well.

125g (4oz) dark chocolate
15g (½ oz) solid white
  vegetable shortening
½ cup cream
1 punnet strawberries
¼ cup strawberry jam
2 teaspoons brandy
CHOCOLATE FILLING
90g (3oz) dark chocolate
1 tablespoon brandy
2 eggs, separated
½ cup cream

Chocolate Filling: Chop chocolate roughly, put into top of double saucepan; stir over hot water until melted. Remove from heat, cool slightly, gradually add brandy and egg yolks. Beat until mixture is smooth and thick. Whip cream lightly, fold into the chocolate mixture. Beat egg whites until soft peaks form. Fold half the egg whites into chocolate mixture, then fold in remaining half. (It's much easier to incorporate egg whites when you fold them in in two portions rather than adding them all at once.)

STEP 1

Lightly grease deep 15cm (6in.) square cake tin. Line tin by placing two strips of aluminium foil crossways in tin. Bring foil up over top of tin, to allow easy removal of the chocolate case when set.

STEP 2

Put chopped chocolate and vegetable shortening in top of double saucepan, stir over gently-simmering water until melted; cool. Pour into foil-lined tin. Move tin around to swirl chocolate around sides and base of tin; try to keep top edges as even as possible. Chocolate should come about 3.5cm (1½in.) up sides of tin. Put into refrigerator for approximately 1 minute to set chocolate slightly. There will be some unset chocolate remaining on base of tin. Move tin around again to swirl this unset chocolate over the set chocolate; this strengthens sides of chocolate box. Refrigerate until set.

STEP 3

Pour chocolate filling into prepared chocolate box; refrigerate until set. Carefully lift chocolate box from tin. Remove foil, place box on serving dish. Whip cream, pipe decoratively around edge of chocolate box. Wash and hull strawberries; drain, cut in half. Pile strawberries over chocolate filling. Put jam and brandy into small saucepan, stir over low heat until melted; push through strainer. Brush strawberries with the strawberry glaze. Refrigerate until ready to serve. □

Potted Seafood
Chicken in a Basket
Julienne of Zucchini
Onion Rings, Potato Straws
Chocolate Ice-cream Log

This dinner party for 4 is easy and delightfully informal. The first course and dessert can be prepared a day beforehand, leaving only the main course for attention on the day of the party

Opposite, clockwise from top left: Onion Rings, Julienne of Zucchini and Potato Straws, Chicken in a Basket, Chocolate Ice-cream Log, Potted Seafood.

POTTED SEAFOOD
500g (1lb) small prawns
170g can crab
4 shallots
1 tablespoon lemon juice
salt, pepper
185g (6oz) butter

Shell prawns, remove black vein; drain crab. Combine in bowl prawns, crab, finely-chopped shallots, lemon juice, salt and pepper. Pack prawn and crab mixture firmly into 4 greased individual dishes. Dot 2 teaspoons of butter on top of prawn mixture in each dish. Put dishes on oven tray, put in moderate oven 10 minutes. Put remaining butter in saucepan, melt over gentle heat until white sediment comes to the top, skim off white sediment and discard. Remove dishes from oven, pour the clarified butter over top of prawn and crab mixture, refrigerate until set. Turn out on to individual serving plates, serve with toast triangles or Melba Toast.   ▷

CHICKEN IN A BASKET

4 x 750g (1½lb) chickens
125g (4oz) butter
salt, pepper
1 cup water
1 chicken stock cube

Put chickens in large baking dish, rub well with softened butter, sprinkle with salt and pepper. Add water and crumbled stock cube to pan. Roast in moderately hot oven 1 hour or until golden brown and cooked. Brush chicken well with pan juices about every 15 minutes during cooking time. Add an extra ½ cup water to pan if water evaporates too quickly. Drain chickens well. Serve each chicken in a small basket lined with paper napkins.

Chicken in a Basket is finger food, so serve finger bowls filled with warm water with a slice of lemon floating in the water. As the water cools, the lemon can be used to remove any grease from fingers. There is a correct way to eat this dish: break off one leg first. Eat this before breaking off any further pieces. In this way, the chicken retains its heat. One hand only should be used to convey the food to the mouth. Rinse fingers often in the finger bowl. Make sure that the napkins are a big size.

JULIENNE OF ZUCCHINI

500g (1lb) zucchini

Wash zucchini, trim ends. Cut zucchini into strips 5cm x 5mm (2in. x ¼in.). Drop zucchini into saucepan of boiling salted water, boil uncovered 2 minutes, rinse under hot water, drain once more.

ONION RINGS

4 onions
1 cup milk
1 egg
1 cup plain flour
¼ teaspoon salt
oil for deep-frying

Peel onions, slice thinly and then separate into rings. Put into bowl, add milk, let stand 1 hour. Drain, reserve milk. Beat egg well, then beat in reserved milk, salt and sifted flour. Dip each onion ring into batter, drop into deep hot oil, a few rings at a time. Fry until golden brown, drain well, sprinkle with salt.

POTATO STRAWS

2 large potatoes
oil for deep-frying

Peel potatoes, cut into 5mm (¼in.) slices, then into strips 5mm (¼in.) wide. Roll chips in clean tea-towel to dry them. Heat oil in deep pan, cook chips 6 minutes, remove, drain well. Before serving, reheat oil, add chips, cook further 3 minutes until golden brown and crisp, drain well, sprinkle with salt.

CHOCOLATE ICE-CREAM LOG

2 litre carton vanilla ice-cream
2 teaspoons instant coffee powder
2 teaspoons coffee liqueur (Tia Maria or Kahlua)
60g (2oz) roasted hazelnuts
¼ cup coconut
1 tablespoon bottled chocolate topping
90g (3oz) dark chocolate
15g (½oz) solid white vegetable shortening

Divide ice-cream evenly into three bowls. Keep in freezer until each is required. Dissolve coffee powder in coffee liqueur, add to one bowl of slightly softened ice-cream. Pour into foil-lined 23cm x 12cm (9in. x 5in.) loaf tin; freeze until firm. Each layer must be firm before topping with the next. Put hazelnuts in blender, blend until finely chopped, stir into the second bowl of slightly softened ice-cream, pour over coffee layer, freeze. Put coconut into heavy-based pan, stir over gentle heat until light golden brown, remove from pan immediately; cool. Add chocolate topping and coconut to remaining slightly softened ice-cream, spread over hazelnut layer. Cover tin with aluminium foil, freeze overnight. Put chopped chocolate and vegetable shortening in top of double saucepan, stir over gently simmering water until melted, cool. Turn ice-cream log on to oven tray. Put chocolate in small plastic bag, snip one corner, drizzle the chocolate decoratively over top and sides of ice-cream log. Put ice-cream log on to serving plate, put in freezer until required. To serve, cut into slices using knife dipped in hot water.

Wine-flavoured camembert can be served with drinks before dinner — Melba Toast or toast triangles are a good accompaniment, or it can be served, as the French serve cheese, before dessert, or it can accompany after-dinner coffee. It is deliciously creamy; the toasted almonds give good texture contrast.

150g can camembert
¾ cup dry white wine
125g (4oz) butter
few drops tabasco
90g (3oz) flaked almonds

STEP 1

Place camembert in small bowl, cover with the wine; cover, leave overnight. Next day, drain off wine, chop camembert roughly — including rind. Put into small bowl of electric mixer. Add softened butter and a few drops of tabasco, beat on medium speed until mixture is smooth and well blended. Refrigerate 5 minutes. Place flaked almonds on oven tray, bake in moderate oven 5 minutes or until pale golden brown; cool. Shape cheese mixture into original shape of cheese.

STEP 2

Roll top and sides of cheese in toasted almonds, patting them on firmly with hands. Refrigerate until firm. Remove from refrigerator 30 minutes before serving. ☐

Chilli Nuts
Korma Curry
Saffron Rice
Dhall, Cucumber Salad
Champagne Sorbet

A curry party has lots of flavour. There are chilli nuts to serve with drinks before dinner, a rich lamb curry for main course and interesting accompaniments. In our picture we show slices of mango — fresh or canned — sliced bananas dipped in lemon juice then rolled in coconut, crisp pappadams. Pappadams can be bought, packaged, in small or large size; drop them, one at a time, into hot oil — hold them down in the oil with a spatula — and let them cook for a minute or two until they become crisp; drain on absorbent paper. The menu serves 6

Opposite, clockwise from top left: Pappadams, Champagne Sorbet, Bananas with Coconut, Chilli Nuts, Dhall, Cucumber Salad, Mango Slices, Saffron Rice, (centre) Korma Curry.

CHILLI NUTS
1 tablespoon oil
1 cup Rice Bubbles
1 cup sultanas
125g (4oz) salted peanuts
125g (4oz) salted cashews
pinch chilli powder

Heat oil in pan, add Rice Bubbles, cook 1 minute. Stir in sultanas, peanuts, cashews, cook over medium heat further 2 minutes, stirring constantly. Remove from heat, stir in chilli powder, cool. Store in an airtight container.

KORMA CURRY
2 x 1.25kg (2½lb) legs of lamb
3 large onions
2 cloves garlic
30g (1oz) ghee or butter
3 tablespoons oil
1 teaspoon grated green ginger
2 tablespoons natural yoghurt
3 tablespoons milk
½ teaspoon cinnamon
pinch ground cloves
1 teaspoon chilli powder
1 teaspoon ground cumin
2 teaspoons ground coriander
1 teaspoon ground cardamom
1½ teaspoons salt
3 bayleaves
3 cups water
pinch nutmeg

Ask butcher to remove bones from legs of lamb. Remove any fat and membrane, cut meat into 2.5cm (1in.) pieces. Peel onions, slice thinly; crush garlic. Heat ghee and oil in pan, add meat gradually, brown well. (Cook meat in about four separate lots; if meat is added too quickly, juices will escape; meat will be dry and will not brown well.) When one lot of meat is well browned all over, remove from pan, continue with remaining meat. Add onions to remaining oil and ghee in pan, cook until light golden brown, stirring constantly; add crushed garlic and ginger, cook a few minutes, add yoghurt and milk, cook further few minutes. Return meat to pan, add cinnamon, cloves, chilli powder, cumin, coriander, cardamom, salt, bayleaves and water, mix well. Cover, ▷

bring to boil, reduce heat, simmer, covered 1 hour; remove lid, cook gently further 30 minutes or until meat is tender and liquid is reduced to desired consistency. Serve sprinkled very lightly with nutmeg.

SAFFRON RICE
1 tablespoon ghee
125g (4oz) blanched almonds
1½ tablespoons ghee, extra
1 onion
2½ cups long grain rice
2 chicken stock cubes
2 cloves
¼ teaspoon cardamom
¼ teaspoon cinnamon
½ teaspoon garam masala
pinch saffron
salt, pepper
1 litre (4 cups) water
½ cup sultanas

Heat ghee in pan, add almonds, fry until golden brown, remove from pan. Add extra ghee to pan; when heated, add peeled and sliced onion, fry until golden brown. Add rice, stir 3 minutes, add crumbled stock cubes, cloves, cardamom, cinnamon, garam masala, saffron, salt, pepper and water, mix well. Bring rice to boil, reduce heat, simmer gently, covered, 15 minutes or until liquid has just been absorbed. Lightly stir in sultanas, cook over very low heat further 7 to 10 minutes. Toss in almonds just before serving.

DHALL
250g (8oz) red lentils
1 teaspoon salt
1 tablespoon curry powder
400g can whole tomatoes
1 onion
2½ cups water
1 clove garlic
2 tablespoons oil

Combine in pan lentils, salt, curry powder, undrained chopped tomatoes, peeled and roughly-chopped onion and water. Bring to boil, reduce heat, cover, simmer 50 to 60 minutes, or until lentils are tender. Pour half the mixture into blender, blend on medium speed 30 seconds. Repeat process with remaining mixture. Stir in crushed garlic and oil.

CUCUMBER SALAD
1 large cucumber
1 onion
salt
2 teaspoons lemon juice

Peel cucumber, score with fork, cut into thin slices; peel onion, slice thinly. Sprinkle salt over cucumber, stand 30 minutes, drain. Combine cucumber, onion and lemon juice, mix well.

CHAMPAGNE SORBET
¼ cup sugar
1 cup water
200ml bottle champagne
2 egg whites
¼ cup sugar, extra

Put sugar and water in saucepan, stir over low heat until sugar is dissolved, cool. Add champagne, pour into deep 20cm (8in.) cake tin, freeze until firm. Beat egg whites until soft peaks form, add extra sugar, beat until sugar is dissolved. Using fork, fold meringue into frozen champagne mixture. Return to freezer, freeze until firm, stirring with fork occasionally. To serve, flake sorbet with fork, spoon over fresh fruit. We used sliced strawberries and kiwi fruit.

Fresh dates, when in season, are delicious prepared this way. When fresh dates are not available, buy packaged dessert dates. Serve the Chocolate Liqueur Dates with a bowl of whipped cream for dipping.

250g (8oz) dates
1 tablespoon finely chopped
**   orange rind**
2 teaspoons Grand Marnier
1 tablespoon ground almonds
45g (1½oz) butter
1 small egg yolk
90g (3oz) dark chocolate
90g (3oz) dark chocolate, extra
15g (½oz) solid white vegetable
**   shortening**

Filling: Place chopped chocolate in top of double saucepan, stand over simmering water until chocolate has melted; put orange rind in small bowl, add Grand Marnier, stand 5 minutes. Cream butter until soft, add egg yolk, mix well. Gradually beat in melted chocolate, stir in orange rind and liqueur and ground almonds, mix well. Refrigerate 10 minutes or until mixture is firm enough to pipe.

STEP 1

Using a sharp knife make a slit down side of date. Remove stone with fingers. Repeat process with remaining dates.

STEP 2

Place prepared filling in small plastic bag. Work filling down to one corner of bag. Snip off corner with scissors. Hold date between thumb and forefinger, press gently to open date, pipe filling down centre of date. Press date closed with fingers. Run the blade of a knife down cut edge of date to smooth off filling. Repeat with remaining dates. Refrigerate 15 minutes.

STEP 3

Melt chopped extra chocolate and vegetable shortening in top of double saucepan over simmering water. Stir to combine. Pour chocolate into small deep glass. Place dates on end of skewer, dip into chocolate.

STEP 4

Shake off excess chocolate, then place on aluminium foil-lined tray. Use another skewer to push date off as shown. Refrigerate until ready to serve. Makes approximately 12.

Note: Excess filling can be piped on to aluminium foil-lined tray, refrigerated until firm, then coated in chocolate to make small individual chocolates. □

Caviar Pate
Fish Fillets with Artichokes
New Potatoes
Beans with Hot Lemon Butter
Rum Plums
with Cinnamon Cream

This dinner party menu is an excellent one for the working woman. Shop for the ingredients on the way home, and you can have the whole meal on the table in no time at all. Preparation is simple, cooking time is short. If you have a blender, fresh breadcrumbs take only seconds to make or you can use packaged dry breadcrumbs. Use canned new potatoes as one of the vegetables; heat, drain, toss in a little melted butter and chopped parsley.
The menu serves 4

Opposite, clockwise from top left: Caviar Pate, Rum Plums with Cinnamon Cream, Fish Fillets with Artichokes, Beans with Hot Lemon Butter, New Potatoes.

CAVIAR PATE
250g (8oz) packet cream cheese
500g (1lb) liverwurst
4 tablespoons tomato sauce
2 teaspoons worcestershire sauce
4 tablespoons dry sherry
salt, pepper
¼ cup sour cream
105g jar red caviar

Place cream cheese in small bowl of electric mixer. Beat until soft and creamy. Add remaining ingredients, except sour cream and caviar, beat until mixture is combined and creamy. Spoon pate into serving bowl or four individual serving bowls. Cover, refrigerate until ready to serve. To serve, place a spoonful of sour cream in centre of pate, spoon caviar around sour cream. Serve with toast triangles. ▷

FISH FILLETS WITH ARTICHOKES

8 bream fillets (or other fillets)
flour
2 eggs
2 tablespoons milk
3 cups fresh breadcrumbs
60g (2oz) butter
2 tablespoons oil

SAUCE

30g (1oz) butter
1 onion
2 tablespoons flour
3 teaspoons french mustard
1 cup milk
½ cup dry white wine
400g can artichoke hearts
½ cup cream
1 tablespoon chopped parsley
salt, pepper

Skin fish, remove bones, coat with flour, dip in combined beaten eggs and milk, coat well with breadcrumbs. Melt butter with oil in large pan, add fish, cook until well browned on both sides. Serve hot with sauce.

Sauce: Melt butter, add peeled and finely-chopped onion, cook until onion is transparent. Add flour and mustard, stir until smooth, remove from heat, add milk and wine. Return to heat, stir over medium heat until sauce boils and thickens. Add drained, sliced artichokes, simmer 2 minutes. Add cream, parsley, salt and pepper, reheat without boiling.

BEANS WITH HOT LEMON BUTTER

500g (1lb) young green beans
60g (2oz) butter
2 tablespoons lemon juice
salt, pepper

Top and tail beans; leave whole. Add beans all at once to large saucepan of boiling salted water, boil uncovered for 5 minutes. Drain and place beans in cold water, leave until cold; drain. Heat butter in pan, add beans, toss in butter for 2 minutes. Add lemon juice, salt and pepper. Toss beans quickly over high heat until all lemon juice has evaporated and beans are well coated in butter.

RUM PLUMS WITH CINNAMON CREAM

2 x 825g cans dark plums
2.5cm (1in.) piece cinnamon stick
4 whole cloves
2 tablespoons rum
300ml carton cream
2 teaspoons sugar
cinnamon

Drain plums, reserve syrup. Cut plums in half, remove stones. Place syrup in pan with cinnamon stick and cloves, bring to boil, reduce heat, simmer uncovered for 5 minutes, remove from heat, add rum, stir until combined; strain syrup over plums. Refrigerate until cold. Spoon plums with syrup into serving bowls. Place cream and sugar into bowl, beat until soft peaks form. Spoon on top of plums, sprinkle with a little cinnamon.

If you're looking for a small, elegant biscuit to serve with after-dinner coffee, this is the one. A rich, buttery shortbread is topped with a crunchy almond toffee, then dipped in chocolate. The recipe makes nearly 30 biscuits.

PASTRY
90g (3oz) butter
2 tablespoons sugar
½ teaspoon vanilla
¾ cup plain flour
TOPPING
30g (1oz) butter
½ cup sugar
⅓ cup slivered almonds
1½ tablespoons cream
1½ tablespoons plain flour
125g (4oz) dark chocolate
30g (1oz) solid white
vegetable shortening

STEP 1
Line a 28cm x 18cm (11in. x 7in.) lamington tin with aluminium foil. Beat butter, sugar and vanilla until light and fluffy. Add sifted flour, mix to a firm dough; knead dough lightly into smooth round shape. Press dough into base of prepared tin, bake in moderate oven 10 minutes.

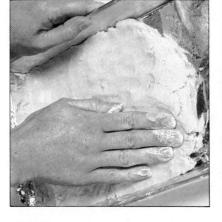

STEP 2
Put butter, sugar, almonds, cream and flour into saucepan, stir over low heat until butter has melted and sugar dissolved.

STEP 3
Spread topping mixture over base, return to moderate oven, bake further 30 to 35 minutes until light golden brown. Remove from oven, loosen edges carefully with knife; cool in tin.

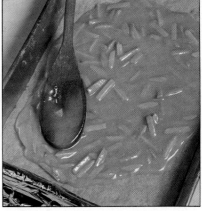

STEP 4
Turn biscuit slice out, cut into 4cm (1½in.) squares. Put chocolate and vegetable shortening in top of double saucepan, stand over simmering water until melted, dip biscuits into chocolate mixture diagonally, so that half the biscuit is coated in chocolate. □

Veal and Broccoli Consomme with Curry Mayonnaise Rusks
Lemon Crumbed Chicken
Potato and Carrot Casserole
Ratatouille
Mangoes with Coconut Rum Ice

You'll like the contrast of flavours and textures provided by each course in this delightful dinner party for 4. The stock for the consomme — which starts this light, delicious meal — can be made the day before; add the rice and so on when reheating it. Make the coconut ice the day before; flake it the next day and return to the freezer, all ready for serving. The Curry Mayonnaise Rusks can be prepared some hours ahead, so that they only have to be heated through; so, too, can the Potato and Carrot Casserole. The chicken can be crumbed, covered and refrigerated beforehand. Vegetables for the Ratatouille can be cut up as directed, put into a plastic bag and refrigerated; but don't cut the eggplant up until just before you are going to cook the vegetables — it can discolour rapidly

Opposite, clockwise from front: Lemon Crumbed Chicken with Ratatouille, Veal and Broccoli Consomme with Curry Mayonnaise Rusks, Potato and Carrot Casserole, and Mangoes with Coconut Rum Ice.

VEAL AND BROCCOLI CONSOMME
1 veal knuckle
1¾ litres (7 cups) water
½ teaspoon cinnamon
500g (1lb) broccoli or 375g (12oz) packet frozen broccoli
2 tablespoons rice
125g (4oz) mushrooms
6 shallots
salt, pepper

Put veal, water and cinnamon in saucepan, bring to boil, reduce heat, simmer covered for 1½ hours. Remove knuckle, discard veal; strain stock twice through fine sieve. Remove stems and leaves from broccoli, cut broccoli into flowerets. (If using frozen broccoli, defrost and cut into small flowerets.) Drop broccoli into boiling salted water, cook 1 minute, drain and rinse under cold running water.

Put veal stock in saucepan, bring to boil, add rice, boil until tender, approximately 10 minutes. Add sliced mushrooms, sliced shallots, broccoli, salt and pepper; reduce heat, simmer 2 minutes. Serve with Curry Mayonnaise Rusks.

CURRY MAYONNAISE RUSKS
6 slices bread
60g (2oz) butter
2 tablespoons mayonnaise
2 teaspoons curry powder
2 tablespoons grated parmesan cheese
salt, pepper
paprika

Remove crusts from bread, toast one side of each slice of bread. Combine softened butter, mayonnaise, curry powder, cheese, salt and pepper. Spread evenly over untoasted side of each slice of bread, sprinkle with paprika. Cut each slice evenly into three. Put on oven tray, bake in moderate oven 15 to 20 minutes or until well browned. ▷

LEMON CRUMBED CHICKEN

4 whole chicken breasts
¼ cup lemon juice
½ cup dry white wine
2 tablespoons oil
salt, pepper
flour
2 eggs
1½ cups packaged dry breadcrumbs
60g (2oz) ground almonds
¼ teaspoon oregano
2 tablespoons chopped parsley
1 teaspoon grated lemon rind
1 tablespoon grated parmesan
   cheese
90g (3oz) butter
1 tablespoon oil, extra
2 teaspoons flour, extra
½ cup cream
1 tablespoon chopped parsley, extra

Remove skin from chicken breasts. Carefully remove chicken meat from bones, giving 8 individual pieces. Gently pound out each chicken breast. Combine lemon juice, wine, oil, salt and pepper, pour over chicken breasts, allow to stand 2 hours. Drain chicken breasts, reserve marinade. Coat chicken lightly in flour seasoned with salt and pepper, dip in beaten eggs, then coat chicken in combined breadcrumbs, ground almonds, oregano, parsley, lemon rind and parmesan cheese. Heat butter and extra oil in large frying pan, add chicken, cook on both sides until golden brown and cooked through, remove from pan, keep warm. Add extra flour to pan, cook 1 minute, add reserved marinade, stir until smooth, bring to boil, reduce heat, simmer 1 minute. Add cream and extra parsley, reheat without boiling. Put chicken on plate, spoon sauce over.

POTATO AND CARROT CASSEROLE

750g (1½lb) potatoes
60g (2oz) butter
¼ cup sour cream
¼ cup milk
salt, pepper
750g (1½lb) carrots
3 chicken stock cubes
1 onion
1 teaspoon french mustard
⅓ cup mayonnaise
30g (1oz) butter, extra
1 tablespoon milk, extra

Peel potatoes, chop roughly. Cook in boiling salted water until tender, drain. Add butter, mash until smooth, add sour cream, milk, salt and pepper, beat until smooth.

Peel carrots, chop roughly, put in saucepan with crumbled stock cubes and peeled and chopped onion. Cover with water, bring to boil, reduce heat, simmer uncovered 15 to 20 minutes or until tender. Drain, reserve 2 tablespoons of the carrot liquid. Put carrot mixture, reserved carrot liquid, salt, pepper, mustard and mayonnaise into electric blender, blend until pureed, or mash until smooth. Put potato and carrot mixtures in layers in ovenproof dish. Dot extra butter over top of casserole, brush with extra milk. Bake in moderate oven 30 to 35 minutes or until top is golden.

RATATOUILLE

1 eggplant
2 red peppers
2 green peppers
3 zucchini
¾ cup oil
2 onions
2 cloves garlic
½ teaspoon thyme
750g (1½lb) tomatoes
salt, pepper

Peel eggplant, cut into large chunks. Remove seeds from peppers, cut into 2.5cm (1in.) cubes, cut zucchini into rounds, peel and chop onions. Heat 2 tablespoons oil in large pan, add onions, crushed garlic and thyme. Cook until onions are transparent, remove from pan. Saute each of the vegetables separately in pan in remaining oil, add to the onion. Peel tomatoes, cut into wedges, add to other vegetables. Put all vegetables in large pan, season with salt and pepper, bring to boil, reduce heat, simmer uncovered 10 to 15 minutes, stirring occasionally.

MANGOES WITH COCONUT RUM ICE

375g (12oz) coconut
½ cup sugar
½ teaspoon salt
1½ litres (6 cups) boiling water
2 x 425g cans mango slices
4 passionfruit
1 tablespoon rum

Put coconut, sugar and salt into bowl, pour boiling water over, stir well, let stand 20 minutes. Strain coconut through fine sieve, then using hands, press out excess liquid from coconut, strain again. Pour coconut liquid into refrigerator trays (the coconut is now discarded), freeze until solid. (Mixture will separate into layers, but reconstitutes perfectly on beating.)

Turn into large bowl of electric mixer, beat on low speed until mixture is mushy and evenly combined. Return to refrigerator trays, freeze again until firm. Drain mangoes. Arrange mangoes in serving dishes, spoon passionfruit pulp over.

Run fork firmly down the coconut ice to break it into flakes. This can be done several hours beforehand and the ice returned to the freezer.

Spoon the flaked ice on top of the fruit and, just before serving, spoon 1 teaspoon of rum over each serving. Or serve the rum in separate liqueur glasses so that guests can pour the rum over before eating.

Note: Of course fresh mango slices can be substituted for the canned in the above recipe. Or, for those who do not like mangoes, strawberries or bananas (still with the passionfruit pulp spooned over) can be substituted.

These delicious little chocolate balls are filled with liqueur ice-cream; they're the perfect accompaniment to after-dinner coffee. Any favourite liqueur can be used — use Grand Marnier or Cointreau for a rich orange flavour, or Kahlua or Tia Maria for a coffee liqueur flavour. The recipe makes about 30.

1 tablespoon gelatine
2 tablespoons water
3 tablespoons liqueur
1 litre carton vanilla ice-cream
125g (4oz) dark chocolate
**60g (2oz) solid white vegetable
   shortening**

Sprinkle gelatine over water, dissolve over hot water, cool; add liqueur. Put ice-cream into small bowl of electric mixer, add gelatine mixture, beat until just combined. (It is important that the gelatine be quite cool but still completely liquid when added to the ice-cream, and that it be beaten into the ice-cream as quickly as possible; otherwise, the gelatine will form lumps in the ice-cream.) Put ice-cream back into container, freeze several hours or overnight until firm.

STEP 1

Before making these ice-cream balls, put an oven tray in the freezer to become very cold. With melon baller, and working quickly, scoop out balls of ice-cream and put on to the cold tray; dip the melon baller into cold water after scooping out each ball. Put the tray with the ice-cream balls back into the freezer, freeze until firm.

STEP 2

Remove ice-cream balls from the freezer, push small wooden sticks into each ice-cream ball at a slight angle (the angle makes for easier eating). Return ice-cream balls to the freezer until firm again.

STEP 3

Put chocolate and vegetable shortening in top of double saucepan. Stand over simmering water until melted, remove from heat, allow to cool slightly. Pour chocolate into small drinking glass, dip ice-cream balls into chocolate, coat well. Put chocolate-coated balls on to cold tray, return to freezer, freeze until firm. ☐

Crab and Salmon Pate
Crumbed Noisettes of Lamb with Mint and Chive Butter
Baked Creamed Potatoes, Salad
Hazelnut Cherry Tart

A delightful fish pate, with the luxury flavour of crab, is the first course of this surprisingly easy dinner party for 4. The main course is tender noisettes of lamb, coated with a chutney mixture, then golden crumbed. The potato accompaniment can be prepared in advance and reheated in the oven just 20 to 30 minutes before you serve it. Dessert is a superb cherry tart with hazelnut pastry

Opposite, top: Baked Creamed Potatoes: below: Crumbed Noisettes of Lamb with Mint and Chive Butter and Salad.

CRAB AND SALMON PATE
60g (2oz) butter
2 tablespoons plain flour
½ cup milk
½ cup cream
⅓ cup dry white wine
salt, pepper
1 teaspoon french mustard
3 teaspoons gelatine
¼ cup water
250g can red salmon
155g can crab

Heat butter in pan, add flour, stir until combined, remove pan from heat. Add milk and cream, stir until combined. Return pan to heat, stir until sauce boils and thickens. Reduce heat, simmer 2 minutes, remove pan from heat. Gradually stir in wine. Season with salt and pepper. Add mustard; mix well. Sprinkle gelatine over water; when softened, add to white sauce mixture. Return pan to heat, stir for 4 minutes, do not boil. Put sauce into electric blender, add drained salmon with bones and any dark skin removed. Blend on medium speed for 2 minutes or until very smooth. Add drained flaked crab; mix well (do not blend). Pour into four individual bowls. Cover bowls, refrigerate several hours or overnight. Serve with Melba Toast (see recipe on page 93). ▷

CRUMBED NOISETTES OF LAMB

8 lamb short loin chops
⅓ cup fruit chutney
2 teaspoons french mustard
salt, pepper
¼ teaspoon thyme
plain flour
4 eggs
packaged dry breadcrumbs
60g (2oz) butter
3 tablespoons oil
MINT AND CHIVE BUTTER
125g (4oz) butter
3 tablespoons chopped mint
2 tablespoons chopped chives
1 tablespoon chopped parsley
salt, pepper

Ask butcher to cut each chop 3cm (1¼in.) thick. Remove bones, or ask butcher to do this for you. Trim any surplus fat from chops. Combine sieved chutney, mustard, salt, pepper and thyme in bowl. Spread chutney mixture evenly over chops, then roll each up firmly into neat round; secure with small wooden stick. Coat chops with flour seasoned with salt and pepper. Dip into beaten eggs, then coat firmly with breadcrumbs. Repeat egg-and-breadcrumb process. Put chops on to tray, refrigerate until ready to cook. Heat butter and oil in large frying pan. Put chops into pan, cook over very low heat until golden brown and cooked through, approximately 8 minutes each side. Drain on absorbent paper. Put on to serving plate, remove sticks, top each with a thick slice of Mint and Chive Butter.

Mint and Chive Butter: Put softened butter and remaining ingredients into bowl, mix well. With wet hands, form into roll approximately 2.5cm (1in.) in diameter. Roll up in greaseproof paper, refrigerate until set and ready to serve.

BAKED CREAMED POTATOES

1 kg (2lb) old potatoes
1 cup mayonnaise
½ cup sour cream
¼ cup milk
2 eggs
2 teaspoons prepared mustard
2 tablespoons chopped parsley
salt, pepper
90g (3oz) cheese
¼ cup grated parmesan cheese

Peel and chop potatoes, cook in boiling salted water until tender, drain well. Mash until smooth, mix with mayonnaise, sour cream, milk, lightly-beaten eggs and mustard; season with salt and pepper. Press mixture through sieve, add parsley, mix well; spoon mixture evenly into greased ovenproof dish. Sprinkle with combined grated cheeses. Bake uncovered in moderate oven 20 to 30 minutes or until golden on top.

PASTRY
½ cup plain flour
pinch salt
60g (2oz) ground roasted hazelnuts
2 tablespoons sugar
60g (2oz) butter
1 egg yolk
2 teaspoons water

FILLING
4 egg yolks
¼ cup sugar
1 teaspoon vanilla
1¾ cups cream
3 teaspoons gelatine
2 tablespoons water

TOPPING
2 x 425g cans black cherries
2 teaspoons gelatine
2 teaspoons rum

PASTRY
STEP 1

Sift flour and salt on to board, add hazelnuts; make a large well in centre. Put sugar in centre, make a well in centre of sugar. Add softened butter, egg yolk and water, work together until creamy. Work in flour mixture with spatula, using cutting motion. With hand, work mixture into a soft dough.

STEP 2

With a lightly-floured hand, press dough out to cover base and sides of greased 23cm (9in.) flan tin. Prick base of pastry. Refrigerate pastry 30 minutes. Bake in moderate oven 15 to 20 minutes or until light golden brown. Allow to cool.

FILLING
STEP 3

Put egg yolks, sugar and vanilla in bowl, beat until thick and creamy. Put cream in saucepan, stir over low heat until almost boiling. Remove from heat immediately. Add cream to egg yolk mixture, beat until combined. Pour cream mixture into top of double saucepan. Stir over simmering water until mixture thickens slightly, approximately 4 minutes. Sprinkle gelatine over cold water, dissolve over hot water, add to cream mixture; mix well. Allow cream mixture to become completely cold before pouring into prepared pastry case. Refrigerate until filling has set.

TOPPING
STEP 4

Drain cherries, reserve 1 cup of the syrup. Arrange pitted cherries over filling. Put reserved syrup, gelatine and rum into saucepan, stir over low heat until gelatine has dissolved. Refrigerate until liquid is the consistency of unbeaten egg white, then spoon liquid evenly over cherries, refrigerate until set. ☐

Chicken and Corn Soup
Spinach Lasagne
Vegetables Julienne, Green Salad
Caramel Lemon Delicious

This economical dinner party menu serves 4. The lasagne can be completely prepared the day before, all ready for the final heating before the party

Opposite, clockwise from left: Spinach Lasagne, Vegetables Julienne, Green Salad.

CHICKEN AND CORN SOUP
2 chicken thighs
4 cups water
1 onion
455g can creamed corn
2 chicken stock cubes
3 shallots
2 teaspoons soy sauce
1 teaspoon grated green ginger
1 egg

Place chicken pieces in small pan, add water and peeled and sliced onion, cover, simmer until chicken is cooked, approximately 20 minutes. Reserve 3 cups of the strained chicken stock. Remove meat from bones, discard skin; chop meat into small pieces. Combine in pan creamed corn, reserved chicken stock, chicken meat, crumbled stock cubes, finely-chopped shallots, soy sauce and green ginger. Bring to boil stirring constantly, reduce heat, simmer 3 minutes. Remove from heat, whisk in lightly-beaten egg.

SPINACH LASAGNE
oil
6 sheets lasagne pasta (see below)
60g (2oz) cheddar cheese
**2 tablespoons grated
  parmesan cheese**
250g packet frozen spinach
⅓ cup cream
MEAT SAUCE
1 onion
1 clove garlic
125g (4oz) mushrooms
500g (1lb) minced steak
salt, pepper
½ teaspoon oregano
1 teaspoon sugar
2 x 440g cans tomato puree
CHEESE SAUCE
60g (2oz) butter
4 tablespoons flour
salt, pepper
pinch nutmeg
2 cups milk
125g (4oz) cheddar cheese
**1 tablespoon grated
  parmesan cheese**

Two-thirds fill a large saucepan with salted water, add 2 teaspoons of oil, cover, bring to boil. When water is boiling rapidly, add one sheet of pasta, allow water to return to boil, wait about 2 minutes, then add another sheet of pasta. If saucepan is large enough, three sheets of pasta can be cooked at one time. It is important to add the pasta gradually and cook only up to three pieces at a time. The oil in the water will help prevent the water boiling over, and prevent pasta sticking together. Boil rapidly, uncovered for about 25 minutes, or until very tender. Have ready a large bowl of cold water to which 2 teaspoons of oil have been added. Carefully lift sheets of pasta from boiling water, lower into cold water. Replenish boiling water, if necessary, cook remaining pasta in same way.

Grate cheddar cheese, mix with parmesan cheese. Place spinach in strainer to thaw. While pasta is cooking, prepare Meat and Cheese Sauces.

Lightly grease a 28cm x 18cm (11in. x 7in.) lamington tin, place tin on oven tray for easier handling.

Carefully lift two pieces of pasta from water, trim pasta so that the sheets fit crossways over base of ▷

tin. Spread evenly with half the Meat Sauce, top with half the Cheese Sauce. Press as much liquid as possible from the thawed spinach, spread evenly over Cheese Sauce. Top with two more pieces of trimmed pasta sheets, spread with Meat Sauce then Cheese Sauce, top with remaining trimmed pasta sheets. Sprinkle top with combined cheeses, bake in moderate oven uncovered 20 minutes. Drizzle top evenly with cream, bake further 10 to 15 minutes or until golden brown. Stand 10 minutes before serving.

Meat Sauce: Peel and finely chop onion, crush garlic, slice mushrooms finely. Place meat in heavy-based frying pan, stir with fork until meat is brown, drain off any excess fat. Add onion, garlic and mushrooms, cook until onion is transparent. Season with salt and pepper, add oregano, sugar and tomato puree. Bring to boil, reduce heat, simmer covered 45 minutes. Uncover, simmer until sauce is thick, about further 15 minutes.

Cheese Sauce: Melt butter, remove from heat, add flour, salt, pepper and nutmeg, blend until smooth. Return to heat, stir constantly for a few minutes. Remove from heat, gradually stir in milk, return to heat, stir constantly until sauce boils and thickens, reduce heat, cook 1 minute. Remove from heat, stir in grated cheddar cheese and parmesan cheese, stir until cheeses melt.

Note: You will need to buy a 375g packet of lasagne pasta, which contains about 14 sheets; only six sheets are needed for this recipe.

VEGETABLES JULIENNE
2 carrots
2 potatoes
4 sticks celery
15g (½oz) butter

Peel carrots and potatoes; string celery; cut all vegetables into 6cm x 5mm (2½in. x ¼in.) strips. Cook carrots and potatoes in boiling salted water 5 minutes; add celery, cook further 2 minutes; drain. Return to saucepan, add butter to vegetables, shake lightly until coated.

GREEN SALAD
1 small white onion
1 cucumber
¼ cup bottled french dressing
2 teaspoons lemon juice
1 teaspoon sugar
salt, pepper
1 lettuce
60g (2oz) black olives

Peel and finely slice onion. Peel cucumber, score well with fork, slice thinly. Combine french dressing, lemon juice, sugar, salt and pepper; mix well. Pour over cucumber and onion slices; allow to stand 15 minutes. Wash lettuce, pat dry, place in salad bowl with cucumber and onion slices, dressing, olives. Toss lightly.

CARAMEL LEMON DELICIOUS
CARAMEL
½ cup sugar
¼ cup water
LEMON DELICIOUS
⅓ cup plain flour
½ cup sugar
60g (2oz) butter
1 teaspoon grated lemon rind
3 tablespoons lemon juice
4 eggs, separated

Caramel: Put sugar and water in saucepan, stir over low heat until sugar has dissolved, brushing down sides of saucepan with a brush dipped in hot water to dissolve any sugar grains. Increase heat, boil gently uncovered until light golden brown. Pour caramel evenly into base of four individual heatproof dishes (small souffle dishes are ideal); swirl dishes to coat base and a little of the sides.

Lemon Delicious: Sift flour into bowl, add sugar. Rub in butter until the mixture resembles coarse breadcrumbs. Add lemon rind, lemon juice and egg yolks, beat well. Beat egg whites until firm peaks form, fold into lemon mixture. Spoon lemon mixture evenly into dishes, stand dishes in baking dish which is filled with enough water to come halfway up sides of dishes. Bake in moderately slow oven 50 minutes or until golden brown on top. Loosen edges of pudding with knife, turn out, top with whipped cream.

1 punnet strawberries
125g (4oz) dark chocolate
15g (½oz) solid white vegetable
shortening

STEP 1

Wash strawberries, dry well. Put chopped chocolate and vegetable shortening in top of double saucepan, stir over simmering water until melted; remove from heat, cool.

STEP 2

Use tongs or fingers to hold the strawberries; dip strawberries into chocolate to coat the bottom half of the strawberry, drain off excess chocolate, put on tray lined with aluminium foil, allow to set.   □

Cheese and Chive Souffle with Celery Croutes
Crumbed Steak with Avocado
Spinach with Basil
Bacon Potatoes
Individual Paris-Brest

This dinner party menu is full of delicious surprises. A light cheese souffle you can prepare in the morning, all ready to pop into the oven before dinner. Steak served with avocado and a richly-flavoured sauce. And a chocolate topped ring of choux pastry with a deliciously creamy filling for dessert. The menu serves 4

Opposite, clockwise from top left: Bacon Potatoes and Spinach with Basil, Individual Paris-Brest, Crumbed Steak with Avocado, Cheese and Chive Souffle with Celery Croutes.

CHEESE AND CHIVE SOUFFLE
125g (4oz) butter
⅓ cup plain flour
salt, pepper
1 cup milk
90g (3oz) cheddar cheese
1 tablespoon grated parmesan cheese
4 eggs, separated
3 tablespoons chopped chives

Melt butter in top part of double saucepan over hot water; remove from heat, sift in flour, salt, pepper, stir until smooth and free from lumps. Stir in milk all at once, return to heat; stir over hot water until smooth and thick. Remove from heat; stir in grated cheeses while still hot, stirring until melted. Allow to cool slightly. Beat egg yolks until pale and fluffy, gradually stir into cheese mixture, using thin-edged metal spoon or spatula. Fold in chives, mix well. Using clean bowl and beaters, beat egg whites until soft moist peaks form. Add half the whites to cheese mixture, folding through carefully with flat spatula; then fold in remaining whites. (Adding whites in two portions like this makes it easier to fold them through the mixture; it also makes sure you do not over-beat mixture, thus breaking down the aeration.) Pour souffle mixture over back of spoon or spatula into four greased individual souffle dishes. Fill souffle dishes to within 1cm (½in.) of top. Place on oven tray. Refrigerate uncovered until ready to serve. Souffles may be refrigerated for up to 24 hours. Bake in moderate oven approximately 30 minutes until light golden brown. Serve immediately, with Celery Croutes. ▷

CELERY CROUTES

4 slices bread
60g (2oz) butter
celery seeds

Remove crusts from bread; cut each slice into 3 fingers. Melt butter in small saucepan. Brush both sides of bread with butter. Place on greased oven tray, sprinkle lightly with celery seeds. Bake in moderate oven 5 to 10 minutes or until golden. Turn croutes and brush with butter during cooking.

CRUMBED STEAK WITH AVOCADO

4 scotch fillet steaks
flour
salt, pepper
2 eggs
3 cups fresh white breadcrumbs
** (approximately ½ loaf bread)**
2 tablespoons chopped parsley
60g (2oz) butter
2 tablespoons oil
1 avocado
MUSTARD SAUCE
3 egg yolks
1 tablespoon lemon juice
salt, pepper
2 teaspoons french mustard
125g (4oz) butter

Remove any fat from each steak. Pound the steaks out to 1cm (½in.) thickness. Coat steaks lightly with flour seasoned with salt and pepper. Dip steaks into lightly–beaten eggs, then coat with combined breadcrumbs and parsley, pressing on firmly. Place steaks on to tray, refrigerate until ready to cook. Heat butter and oil in large frying pan, cook steaks until golden brown and cooked to desired degree. Remove from pan, keep warm. Place steaks on to serving plates, place two slices of avocado on each steak, spoon over prepared Mustard Sauce.

Mustard Sauce: Place egg yolks, lemon juice, salt, pepper and mustard into top of double saucepan, stir until combined. Add chopped, softened butter, mix well. Place saucepan over simmering water, stir until sauce is thick and creamy. Remove from heat.

SPINACH WITH BASIL

1 bunch spinach
2 cups parsley sprigs
2 teaspoons fresh basil (or ½
** teaspoon dry basil)**
3 tablespoons oil
1 tablespoon lemon juice
3 tablespoons bottled french dressing

Wash spinach, remove stalks, tear into large pieces. Put parsley sprigs, basil, oil, lemon juice and french dressing in blender, blend until smooth (if necessary, turn off motor and push mixture down from sides of blender). Put parsley mixture into large saucepan, bring to boil, add spinach, toss to coat well with sauce.

BACON POTATOES

4 medium potatoes
1 tablespoon sour cream
1 tablespoon mayonnaise
salt, pepper
¼ teaspoon french mustard
1 egg yolk
2 rashers bacon
30g (1oz) butter

Scrub potatoes well under cold running water; dry well. Place on baking tray, bake in moderate oven for 60 minutes or until potatoes are tender. With serrated knife, carefully cut top off each potato. Scoop potato out with small spoon, leaving 5mm (¼in.) of potato inside to form shell. Push scooped-out potato through sieve. Add sour cream, mayonnaise, salt, pepper, mustard and egg yolk; mix well. Fill potato mixture back into potato shells. Spoon melted butter over the potatoes.

Place potatoes on to oven tray, bake in moderate oven 20 minutes or until heated through.

Remove rind from bacon, chop finely. Place into pan, stir over heat until bacon is crisp; drain. Spoon bacon on top of each potato.

½ cup water
30g (1oz) butter
pinch salt
½ cup plain flour
2 eggs
FILLING
1 egg, separated
1 egg yolk, extra
⅓ cup castor sugar
1 cup milk
1 tablespoon flour
1 tablespoon cornflour
1 teaspoon vanilla
TOPPING
125g (4oz) dark chocolate
30g (1oz) butter
60g (2oz) flaked almonds

Filling: Put egg yolks, 3 tablespoons sugar, ¼ cup milk, sifted flour and cornflour into blender, blend on low speed until mixture is smooth, or beat well until smooth. Put remaining milk in pan, bring to boil, add to egg mixture, blend or beat for 30 seconds. Pour mixture into pan, stir over low heat until mixture boils. (Lumps may form during cooking; however the cream will become smooth with beating when the mixture boils and thickens.) Remove from heat, cool. Whip egg white until soft peaks form, add remaining sugar gradually, beat until firm peaks form. Fold the egg white into the cooled cream, add vanilla, mix well.

STEP 1

Put water, butter and salt in pan. Bring to boil, add sifted flour all at once. Stir vigorously with wooden spoon over heat until mixture is thick. When mixture forms a smooth ball and leaves sides of pan, remove from heat, place pastry on saucer, spread out with back of wooden spoon, leave for 10 minutes. Place cooled pastry in small bowl of electric mixer, add beaten eggs, a little at a time, beating thoroughly after each addition. Mixture should be smooth and glossy.

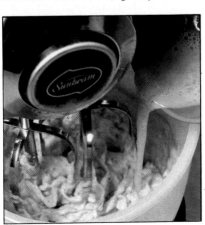

STEP 2

Line oven tray with a sheet of greased greaseproof paper, mark four 8cm (3in.) circles on the paper. Fill pastry into piping bag fitted with 1cm (½in.) plain nozzle. Pipe choux pastry around edge of circles. Bake in hot oven 10 minutes, reduce heat to moderate, bake further 15 to 20 minutes or until dry. Using a sharp knife, cut pastry rings in half horizontally. Return the pastry rings to oven, leave for a few minutes to dry out.

Note: Remaining pastry can be piped into individual choux puffs. Bake in hot oven 10 minutes, reduce heat to moderate, bake further 15 to 20 minutes or until dry. These can be frozen for future use.

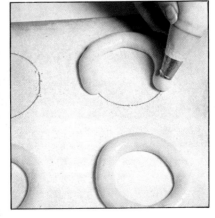

STEP 3

Stand pastry rings on wire rack until completely cold. Spoon prepared filling into piping bag fitted with 1cm (½in.) plain nozzle. Pipe cream evenly into bottom half of each pastry ring.

STEP 4

Combine chopped chocolate and butter in top of double saucepan. Stand over simmering water until chocolate and butter have melted. Stir lightly to combine. Spread chocolate evenly over top halves of rings. Put almonds on baking tray, bake in moderate oven 5 minutes; cool. Sprinkle almonds over tops of chocolate rings. Refrigerate pastry rings until chocolate is firm. Put chocolate rings evenly on top of filled bases. ☐

Salmon Pate
Steak Diane
Bean Bundles, Herbed Tomatoes
Cauliflower au Gratin
Mango Liqueur Pancakes

This simple, elegant dinner party is one that takes little time and trouble to put together. The creamy pate, mixed in a blender, can be prepared the day before, so, too, can the Cauliflower au Gratin — all ready for final reheating in the oven. The pancakes can be made the day before and then gently reheated in the sauce. The menu serves 4

Opposite, from left: Salmon Pate, Cauliflower au Gratin, Steak Diane with Bean Bundles and Herbed Tomatoes.

SALMON PATE
½ cup hot water
1 tablespoon gelatine
1 chicken stock cube
220g can red salmon
4 shallots
¼ cup mayonnaise
2 teaspoons lemon juice
salt, pepper
½ cup cream
lettuce leaves

Put hot water, gelatine and crumbled stock cube in blender, blend on high speed 1 minute. Add undrained salmon, roughly-chopped shallots, mayonnaise, lemon juice, salt and pepper, blend further 1 minute. Add cream, blend 30 seconds. Pour salmon mixture into 4 individual lightly-oiled dishes, refrigerate until set. To serve, turn out on to lettuce leaf, serve with toast triangles. ▷

STEAK DIANE

4 fillet steaks
freshly-ground pepper
60g (2oz) butter
2 cloves garlic
2 tablespoons worcestershire sauce
2 tablespoons cream
2 tablespoons chopped parsley

Pound steaks to 5mm (¼in.) thickness. Season each side lightly with freshly-ground pepper. Put butter into shallow pan; when sizzling, add steaks, cook for 1 minute. Then give steaks a move in the pan so they won't stick. While steaks are cooking on one side, rub crushed garlic into top of each steak with wooden spoon, turn steak over. Add worcestershire sauce to pan, swirl steaks around in the pan juices. When cooked as desired — rare, medium or well done — quickly stir in cream and chopped parsley. Serve immediately.

BEAN BUNDLES

500g (1lb) beans
chives
60g (2oz) butter
1 tablespoon lemon juice
salt, pepper

Top, tail and string beans. Put into boiling salted water; cook until just tender, approximately 10 minutes, drain. Divide beans into four bunches; secure each bunch with chives. Melt butter in pan; add lemon juice; stir until combined. Add beans; heat through gently. Season with salt and pepper.

HERBED TOMATOES

4 tomatoes
1 tablespoon lemon juice
salt, pepper
15g (½oz) butter
2 teaspoons chopped parsley
1 teaspoon chopped chives
1 teaspoon basil

Slice off stem end of each tomato; put tomatoes into greased ovenproof dish. Sprinkle lemon juice over cut top of tomatoes, then salt and pepper. Bake in moderate oven 10 minutes. Remove from oven, dot each tomato with butter; sprinkle combined parsley, chives and basil over; bake for a further 5 minutes.

MANGO LIQUEUR PANCAKES

PANCAKES
½ cup plain flour
pinch salt
2 eggs
¾ cup milk
FILLING
125g (4oz) butter
4 tablespoons sugar
⅔ cup orange juice
2 teaspoons lemon juice
2 tablespoons Cointreau
** or Grand Marnier**
2 tablespoons brandy
2 x 470g cans sliced mangoes

Pancakes: Sift dry ingredients into bowl, add eggs, stir until mixture is smooth and free of lumps. Gradually add milk, mix to a smooth batter. Allow to stand for 30 minutes. Heat pan, grease well. From a small jug pour 2 to 3 tablespoons of pancake mixture into pan, swirling batter evenly around pan. Cook over medium heat until light golden brown. Toss or turn pancake, cook on other side. Repeat with remaining batter.

Filling: Melt butter in frying pan, add sugar, stir until sugar is golden brown, add orange juice and lemon juice, stir until sugar has dissolved. Add Cointreau or Grand Marnier and brandy, set aflame. When flames die, simmer sauce gently 2 minutes, remove pan from heat. Drain mango slices, cut into small cubes. Divide mango pieces between pancakes, fold each pancake in half, then into quarters. Place into sauce, return pan to heat, simmer 2 minutes or until pancakes are heated through, spooning sauce over pancakes.

Top, if desired, with a scoop of vanilla ice-cream.

48

1 small cauliflower
45g (1½oz) butter
3 tablespoons flour
1½ cups milk
60g (2oz) cheddar cheese
salt, pepper
½ cup fresh breadcrumbs
30g (1oz) cheddar cheese, extra
15g (½oz) butter, extra

STEP 1

Remove stalk from cauliflower, cut cauliflower into large flowerets. Cook in boiling salted water until tender, remove from heat, drain.

STEP 2

Put butter in pan, stir over medium heat until melted. Add flour, stir until smooth, cook 1 minute. Add milk gradually, stir until smooth, stir until sauce boils and thickens. Remove from heat, add grated cheese, salt and pepper, stir until cheese melts.

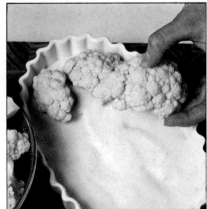

STEP 3

Spread half cheese sauce over base of ovenproof dish, arrange cauliflower on top of sauce, spread remaining sauce over cauliflower.

STEP 4

Combine breadcrumbs, extra grated cheese and extra melted butter. Sprinkle crumb mixture on top of cauliflower. Bake in moderate oven 15 to 20 minutes or until golden brown. □

Scallops en Brochette
Saffron Rice
Duck with Mangoes
Green Peas, Mashed Potatoes
Shallot Buns
Ginger Gelato

Tasmanian scallops for starters, with duck and mangoes to follow, could well form the basis for an Australian menu to serve guests from abroad. Ginger-flavoured gelato rounds off the meal.
The menu serves 4.
Cooking time for the first course of this dinner party is only a few minutes. The main course can be cooked the day before to the point where the ducks are placed in individual casseroles; complete cooking on night of dinner party. Prepare the Shallot Buns the day before, wrap in aluminium foil and refrigerate. The Ginger Gelato also can be made the day before

Opposite, clockwise from top left: Duck with Mangoes and Green Peas and Mashed Potatoes, Shallot Buns, Ginger Gelato, Scallops en Brochette and Saffron Rice.

SCALLOPS EN BROCHETTE
500g (1lb) scallops
butter
lemon juice
salt, pepper
lemon wedges
parsley
   Wash and trim scallops, thread on bamboo skewers. Allow 4 to 6 scallops for each skewer. Brush with melted butter, sprinkle with lemon juice, salt and pepper. Put under hot griller 3 to 4 minutes or until scallops are just golden brown; turn and cook other side, basting with melted butter. Serve on bed of hot saffron rice, garnish with lemon and parsley.   ▷

SAFFRON RICE

½ teaspoon salt
¼ teaspoon saffron
¼ cup long grain rice
30g (1oz) butter

Put a large saucepan of water on to boil, add salt and saffron; when boiling, gradually add rice, cook 12 minutes or until tender. Drain rice well, stir in butter, mix butter through rice until melted.

SHALLOT BUNS

4 round individual buns
125g (4oz) butter
4 shallots
2 tablespoons chopped parsley
1 teaspoon french mustard
salt, pepper

Make four equal cuts in each bun, cutting just to bottom crust, but not right through. Beat butter in bowl until light and creamy. Add finely-chopped shallots, parsley and mustard, mix well. Season with salt and pepper. Spread butter mixture on both sides of bun slices. Wrap each bread bun in aluminium foil. Put in moderate oven for 10 minutes.

GINGER GELATO

345g jar of preserved ginger
1 cup sugar
2 tablespoons lemon juice
4¾ cups water
300ml carton cream

Put ginger with the syrup from jar in blender, blend on high speed until mixture is smooth (or chop ginger finely and combine with syrup). In large saucepan put sugar, lemon juice, water and ginger mixture. Bring slowly to boil, stirring until sugar has dissolved. Boil 15 minutes, remove from heat, cool. When quite cold, stir in whipped cream, pour into refrigerator trays and freeze. When the cream is added to the ginger syrup, the mixtures do not immediately combine. However, while freezing, stir the mixture with a fork frequently. When ice is set, flake with a fork. Kiwi fruit make a colourful decoration.

2 x 1.5kg (3lb) ducks
60g (2oz) butter
½ cup flour
2 cups water
1 cup dry white wine
2 tablespoons port
½ cup Grand Marnier
2 tablespoons brandy
½ cup orange juice
salt, pepper
1 bayleaf
pinch thyme
470g can mango slices

STEP 1

Wash and dry ducks, put into baking dish. Secure vents with small skewers to keep in good shape. Brush each duck with melted butter. Bake in moderately hot oven 60 minutes or until golden brown; brush ducks frequently with melted butter.

STEP 2

Remove ducks from pan, drain all fat from pan; reserve fat. Put baking dish on top of stove, stand over high heat until pan drippings have turned golden brown. Add ½ cup reserved fat, remove pan from heat, add flour, stir until combined. Return pan to heat, stir until flour is dark golden brown; do not allow to burn. Add water, wine, port, Grand Marnier, brandy and orange juice, stir until sauce boils and thickens. Season with salt and pepper. Add bayleaf and thyme, stir until combined.

STEP 3

Put ducks into individual casserole dishes or one large casserole dish. Pour sauce over, cover, bake in moderate oven 1½ hours or until ducks are tender. Remove ducks from pan, cut in half lengthwise, put on to serving plates, pour sauce over. Meanwhile, heat mangoes in their own liquid, drain, serve with ducks. ☐

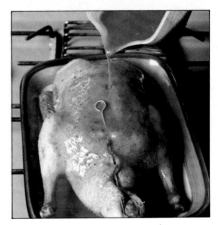

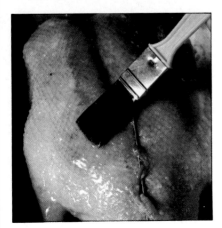

Mussel Soup
Chicken with Green Peppercorns
Braised Celery
Sauteed Mushrooms
Strawberry Whip

The food is delicious, and the kilojoule count is low in this dinner party menu for 4. With three satisfying courses, the kilojoule count is around 2400 — that's 600 calories — per person

Opposite: Sauteed Mushrooms, Chicken with Green Peppercorns, and Braised Celery.

MUSSEL SOUP
250g (8oz) fish fillets
1½ litres (6 cups) water
15g (½oz) butter
2 tablespoons flour
2 teaspoons curry powder
2 tablespoons tomato paste
2 chicken stock cubes
2 tomatoes
16 mussels
salt, pepper
2 tablespoons chopped parsley

Put fish fillets into saucepan, add water, bring to boil, reduce heat, simmer covered 15 minutes. Drain, reserve stock and fish. Melt butter in saucepan, add flour and curry powder, stir until smooth. Add tomato paste, add fish stock gradually, stir until smooth, stir until soup boils and thickens. Add crumbled stock cubes and peeled and chopped tomatoes, simmer 1 minute. Add flaked fish and cleaned mussels, cook further 5 minutes or until mussels open (discard any mussels that do not open). Season with salt and pepper. Spoon into serving bowls, top with chopped parsley. ▷

CHICKEN WITH GREEN PEPPERCORNS

2 whole chicken breasts
30g (1oz) butter
salt, pepper
1 tablespoon lemon juice
2 tablespoons canned green
** peppercorns**
15g (½oz) butter, extra
2 egg yolks
¼ cup cream
2 tablespoons sour cream
1 teaspoon french mustard

Remove chicken breasts from bones, remove skin. Melt butter and place in small baking dish, arrange chicken breasts in dish, sprinkle with salt, pepper and lemon juice. Cover dish with aluminium foil, bake in moderately hot oven 15 minutes or until chicken is tender (cooking time will depend on thickness of chicken breasts). While chicken is cooking, drain peppercorns and rinse under warm water. Heat extra butter in small pan, add peppercorns and cook 1 minute.

Remove chicken breasts from baking dish, arrange on serving platter, keep warm. Reduce remaining pan drippings to 1 tablespoon by simmering over gentle heat for 1 to 2 minutes. Add pan drippings to peppercorns along with combined egg yolks, cream, sour cream and mustard. Stir over low heat until sauce thickens; do not boil; add salt and pepper. Spoon sauce over chicken.

BRAISED CELERY

6 sticks celery
30g (1oz) butter
1 clove garlic
1 chicken stock cube
2 tablespoons water
salt, pepper

String celery, cut into thin diagonal slices. Heat butter in large pan, add crushed garlic and celery, toss in butter mixture 3 minutes. Add crumbled stock cube and water, bring to boil, reduce heat, simmer covered 3 minutes. Remove lid, cook over high heat to evaporate liquid. Season with salt and pepper.

SAUTEED MUSHROOMS

250g (8oz) small mushrooms
30g (1oz) butter
2 shallots
1 tablespoon chopped parsley

Trim stalks of mushrooms, saute mushrooms in hot butter until golden brown. Add finely-chopped shallots and parsley, stir until combined.

STRAWBERRY WHIP

1 punnet strawberries
½ x 225g carton non-fat natural
** yoghurt**
2 tablespoons skim milk
2 teaspoons sugar
1 teaspoon gelatine
2 teaspoons water
1 egg white

Wash and hull strawberries, put 5 into each serving glass. Put remaining strawberries (there should be 11 or 12 strawberries remaining) in blender with yoghurt, milk, and sugar; blend until smooth or beat well with rotary beater. Sprinkle gelatine over water; when softened, dissolve over hot water; cool. Add to strawberry mixture; mix well. Fold in softly-beaten egg white. Spoon mixture over strawberries. Garnish each dish, if desired, with a strawberry half.

Cappuccino is not generally served with dinner, but if the guests linger on, you might like to serve this popular drink before they depart. True Cappuccino needs an expensive machine to make it correctly; this simple method gives a very similar result. For Vienna Coffee, simply top with whipped cream, sprinkle with cinnamon or nutmeg. Quantities given serve 4.

3 cups strong black coffee
⅓ cup cream
cocoa

STEP 1
Place coffee in pan, pour in cream. Bring coffee to a slow boil.

STEP 2
Pour half the coffee mixture into blender, blend on medium speed 30 seconds, pour into two cups. Repeat process with remaining coffee, pour coffee into cups. Sprinkle a little cocoa over top of each coffee cup.   □

Taramasalata
Dolmades and Hors d'Oeuvre
Crisp Rolls
Lamb Kapama
Spinach Rice
Greek Custard Slice
Diples

This dinner party of Greek foods starts with a colourful hors d'oeuvre platter, then there's a lamb casserole served with spinach-flecked rice. There's the popular firm custard slice for dessert and we've added the traditional Greek pastry — Diples — to serve with coffee, or Diples could be served for dessert in place of the custard slice. The name Diples is taken from the Greek "to multiply". The dough is folded several times, hence the name, and the wish that "one's years be multiplied many times over". This menu serves 6

Opposite, front from left:
Lamb Kapama, Hors d'Oeuvre
Platter with Taramasalata,
Dolmades, Spinach Rice (behind).

TARAMASALATA
250g (8oz) old potatoes
6 thick slices white bread
100g can tarama
   or 60g (2oz) fresh tarama
freshly ground pepper
¾ cup lemon juice
½ cup olive oil

Peel, wash and quarter potatoes. Place in boiling water, reduce heat, simmer covered 15 to 20 minutes or until potatoes are tender; drain well. Allow to cool. Remove crusts from bread slices, place bread in large bowl with 1 cup warm water, allow to stand 5 minutes. Place bread in large strainer; press with hand to extract as much water as possible. Place tarama, potatoes, bread and pepper in electric blender or food processor; blend until smooth, or beat together well. Gradually blend in combined lemon juice and olive oil; blend until combined and very smooth. Spoon mixture into serving bowls, cover and refrigerate several hours. Serve with crisp rolls.

Note: Fresh tarama (smoked cod's roe) is available from Greek delicatessens. Our hors d'oeuvre platter contains the taramasalata, a crisp lettuce leaf holding black olives, tomato and cucumber chunks, feta cheese, wedges of lemon or lime.   ▷

DOLMADES

18 vine leaves (see below)
⅓ cup uncooked rice
1 small onion
250g (8oz) minced steak
1 tablespoon chopped parsley
2 tablespoons oil
salt, pepper
pinch cinnamon

Wash leaves under cold water, pat dry. Wash rice, drain well. Peel and finely chop onion, combine with minced steak, parsley, rice and oil, cinnamon, salt and pepper; mix well. Place dessertspoonfuls of mixture into centre of each leaf, roll up into neat parcels. Place rolls in saucepan, packed close together; rolls can be cooked in a double layer. Place a plate or saucer on top of rolls — this will prevent them from unrolling during cooking. Add enough cold water to pan to barely cover rolls. Bring to boil, covered, reduce heat, simmer 1 hour.

Note: Vine leaves can be bought fresh from most Greek delicatessens or fruit shops, or they can be bought in cans or packages. If you buy them in cans or packages, any remaining can be frozen for future use. Rinse vine leaves well and pat dry before you use them.

LAMB KAPAMA

1.5kg (3lb) lamb leg chops
1 tablespoon oil
3 tomatoes
½ cup water
¼ teaspoon cinnamon
1 teaspoon sugar
salt, pepper
¼ teaspoon oregano
3 potatoes
2 sticks celery
2 tablespoons chopped parsley

Remove excess fat from chops, remove bones. Chop chops into large pieces. Heat oil in pan, add lamb, brown well, remove from pan. Pour excess fat from pan. Peel and chop tomatoes, add to pan with water, cinnamon, sugar, salt, pepper and oregano, mix well. Add meat to pan, simmer covered 20 minutes. Add peeled, chopped potatoes, simmer covered further 30 to 40 minutes or until potatoes and meat are tender. Slice celery, cook in boiling salted water 4 minutes, rinse under cold running water, add to lamb 5 minutes before serving. Stir in parsley.

SPINACH RICE

60g (2oz) butter
2 cloves garlic
1½ cups long grain rice
2½ cups water
salt, pepper
6 stalks spinach

Heat butter in pan, add crushed garlic and rice, stir to coat rice with butter, add water, salt and pepper. Bring to boil, reduce heat, simmer very gently uncovered until liquid has almost been absorbed, approximately 10 minutes; stir occasionally. Wash spinach, remove leaves, chop leaves finely, stir into rice. Continue cooking very gently further 5 minutes.

GREEK CUSTARD SLICE

500g (1lb) packet phylo pastry
185g (6oz) butter or substitute
1½ cups sugar
1½ cups water
2 strips lemon rind
¼ cup lemon juice
2 tablespoons honey
CUSTARD
2 litres (8 cups) milk
1½ cups semolina
4 eggs
1¼ cups sugar
1½ teaspoons vanilla

Make custard first to allow time for it to become cold before using. Put milk into a large pan, bring to simmering point, remove from heat immediately. Gradually sprinkle semolina over milk, stirring constantly. Return to heat, stir until mixture boils and thickens. Reduce heat, simmer uncovered 5 minutes, stirring constantly. Remove pan from heat, allow to cool slightly. Beat eggs until combined, add sugar and vanilla, mix well. Gradually add egg mixture to milk mixture, mix well; cool.

Lay phylo pastry out flat. Place a 25cm x 28cm (10in. x 11in.) baking dish on top of the pastry. Using this dish as a guide, cut around baking dish through pastry sheets, cutting pastry 1cm (½in.) larger than the dish. Melt butter over gentle heat; grease baking dish well, then lay one sheet of pastry on the base, brush well with melted butter. Continue layering pastry and brushing with melted butter until half the pastry is used. Pour cold custard over the top of the pastry used, spreading out evenly. Place another sheet of pastry on top of the custard, brush with melted butter; repeat with remaining pastry and butter, brush top of pastry well with butter. Place dish in refrigerator until very cold. With a sharp knife cut through pastry to base, first cutting into 8cm (3in.) squares, then into triangles. Bake in hot oven 15 minutes, reduce heat to moderate, cook a further 40 minutes or until dark golden brown. Remove from oven, re-mark the triangles. Meanwhile, place sugar, water, lemon rind and juice and honey into pan, stir over low heat until sugar has dissolved. Bring to boil, boil uncovered 3 minutes. Remove lemon rind from syrup, allow to cool. Spoon cold syrup over the hot pastry, allowing it to soak in between triangles. Allow to cool, then refrigerate overnight.

**1½ cups plain flour
2 large eggs
pinch salt
1½ teaspoons oil
oil for deep-frying, extra
1½ tablespoons water
4 tablespoons honey
cinnamon**

STEP 1

Sift flour; beat eggs until thick and foamy, gradually beat in sifted flour and salt. When mixture reaches the point where it is too stiff to beat further, work in by hand enough of the remaining flour to give a firm dough.

STEP 2

Turn dough out on to unfloured surface, knead until dough is smooth. Make a dent in the dough, add oil, then work in with your hands until the dough is smooth.

STEP 3

Roll out dough on well-floured board; dough should be paper-thin. Cut into eight 10cm x 15cm (4in. x 6in.) rectangles.

STEP 4

Drop one pastry into deep hot oil. As soon as pastry turns white and bubbles up, remove from oil, place on absorbent paper.

STEP 5

With the aid of two forks, roll up the pastry quickly.

STEP 6

Holding pastry with forks, return to hot oil; use one fork to hold pastry against side of pan for 30 seconds before releasing so that Diple does not unroll. Turn once in oil, to brown, then drain on absorbent paper. Repeat with remaining pastries. Store in air-tight container until ready to serve.

To serve: Heat together water and honey, then dribble over Diples. Sprinkle cinnamon over top. ☐

Crudites with Hot Garlic Dip
Braised Pork with Calvados
Red Cabbage, Green Peas
Hot Potato Casserole
Strawberry Palmiers

This dinner party for 6 is colourful and full of flavour. Vegetables for the first course can be prepared beforehand, covered with plastic food wrap and refrigerated; sauce for the vegetables can also be prepared ahead and gently reheated. For the main course, the red cabbage can also be cooked ahead and gently reheated; the potato casserole can be cooked, ready for final reheating. Palmiers for dessert can be made the day before then filled and decorated before serving

Opposite, clockwise from left: Crudites with Hot Garlic Dip, Green Peas, Braised Pork with Calvados, Red Cabbage, Hot Potato Casserole (back) and Strawberry Palmiers.

CRUDITES WITH HOT GARLIC DIP
3 large carrots
3 sticks celery
1 small cauliflower
1 large cucumber
3 large tomatoes
500g (1lb) mushrooms
2 red peppers
2 green peppers
HOT GARLIC DIP
2 x 300ml cartons cream
3 teaspoons cornflour
¼ cup water
60g (2oz) butter
2 cloves garlic
1 small onion
45g can anchovies
pepper

Peel carrots, trim ends, slice carrots thinly lengthwise; cut celery into strips the same length as carrots; cut cauliflower into flowerets; cut cucumber in half, scoop out seeds, cut into strips the same length as celery and carrot; cut tomatoes into wedges; cut stems off mushrooms; cut peppers in half, remove seeds, cut peppers into large chunks. Put carrots, celery, cauliflower and peppers into rapidly boiling water, boil 2 minutes, drain and rinse immediately under cold running water. Arrange vegetables on individual serving plates, serve with Hot Garlic Dip.

Hot Garlic Dip: Put cream into saucepan, bring to boil, reduce heat, simmer uncovered 10 minutes. Blend cornflour into water, add to cream, stir until cream boils and thickens; remove from heat. Melt butter in frying pan, add crushed garlic and peeled and finely-chopped onion, saute until onion is transparent. Add drained and mashed anchovies and cream, stir over medium heat until sauce boils, reduce heat, simmer uncovered 10 minutes. Season with pepper.

BRAISED PORK WITH CALVADOS
2kg (4lb) loin of pork
2 teaspoons oil
salt, pepper
⅓ cup long grain rice
60g (2oz) butter
1 medium onion
2 sticks celery
¼ cup fresh white breadcrumbs
¼ teaspoon grated lemon rind
2 tablespoons chopped parsley
½ teaspoon basil
1 egg
30g (1oz) butter, extra
4 tablespoons flour
2 cups water
1½ cups dry white wine
¼ cup Calvados or brandy
2 chicken stock cubes
1 teaspoon sugar

Order pork with long flap so that it holds stuffing securely. Ask butcher to remove bones from loin, also to remove rind from fat and to score rind well. Place rind on to large baking tray, rub well with the oil and 1 teaspoon of

salt. Place into very hot oven for 15 to 20 minutes or until rind is well crackled. Remove from oven, pour off all fat from baking tray. When crackling is cold, break or chop crackling into 5cm (2in.) cubes.

Gradually add rice to large saucepan of boiling salted water, boil uncovered for 12 minutes or until rice is tender; drain. Heat butter in pan, add peeled, chopped onion and ▷

finely-chopped celery, saute gently until onion is transparent. Remove pan from heat, add rice, breadcrumbs, lemon rind, salt, pepper, parsley, basil and egg; mix well.

Open loin of pork, fat side down, on board, put prepared stuffing along centre of pork, forming a roll. Roll up, secure with string at 5cm (2in.) intervals.

Heat extra butter in baking dish on top of stove, add pork, brown well on all sides, remove pork from dish. Pour off excess fat, leaving approximately 4 tablespoons of fat in baking dish. Add flour, stir until flour is dark golden brown, remove pan from heat. Add water, wine, Calvados, crumbled stock cubes, sugar, salt, pepper; stir until combined. Return pan to heat, stir until sauce boils and thickens. Return pork to baking dish, spoon sauce over. Cover baking dish tightly with lid or aluminium foil. Bake in moderate oven for 2 hours, spoon sauce over occasionally. To serve pork, place on to hot serving dish with crackling. Skim off any fat that may have formed on top of sauce, serve sauce separately.

Note: Calvados (apple brandy) adds a delicious flavour of its own to the sauce. However, if unavailable, brandy can be substituted.

RED CABBAGE
½ **red cabbage**
30g (1oz) lard
60g (2oz) bacon
1 medium onion
3 tablespoons sugar
½ **cup white vinegar**
1 apple
¾ **cup water**
1 bayleaf
1 teaspoon salt
pepper

Finely shred cabbage, discarding any coarse leaves. Melt lard in large saucepan, add chopped bacon and peeled and chopped onion, cook until onion is golden. Add sugar, cook over medium heat 1 minute. Add shredded cabbage, vinegar, peeled, cored and chopped apple; cover, simmer gently 10 minutes, turning occasionally. Stir in water, bayleaf, salt and pepper, cover; simmer gently further 1½ hours.

HOT POTATO CASSEROLE
750g (1½lb) old potatoes
60g (2oz) butter
1 onion
⅓ **cup sour cream**
2 tablespoons milk
salt, pepper
paprika

Peel and chop potatoes, cook in boiling salted water until tender; drain. Mash well. Melt butter in pan, add peeled and chopped onion, cook until onion is transparent, add to potato with sour cream and milk, mix until smooth, season with salt and pepper. Spoon potato mixture into ovenproof dish, sprinkle with paprika, bake in moderate oven for 15 minutes.

castor sugar
375g (12oz) packet puff pastry
300ml carton cream
1 punnet strawberries

STEP 1

Dust board lightly with castor sugar. Roll out pastry into oblong approximately 15cm x 25cm (6in. x 10in.); trim edges. Sprinkle lightly with castor sugar. Fold the long sides of the pastry in so that they meet edge to edge in the centre.

STEP 2

Bring folds over again so that there are now four even layers of pastry.

STEP 3

Using sharp knife, cut pastry into 1cm (½in.) pieces. Brush one side with water, sprinkle with castor sugar. Put on lightly-greased oven tray, sugar-side up, allow room for spreading. Spread them open at folded ends to make small V. Refrigerate 10 minutes. Bake in hot oven 15 minutes or until crisp and golden. Halfway through cooking time, turn, allow second side to brown and crisp. Cool. Spread whipped cream over one side of half the biscuits, arrange sliced strawberries over cream, top with another biscuit. Pipe the cream decoratively on top of biscuits, decorate with a strawberry. Brush strawberries with warmed, sieved strawberry jam to glaze. ☐

Golden Oat Trout with Parsley Lemon Butter
Scottish Mutton Pie
Spinach Dumplings, Buttered Vegetables
Whisky Oranges with Atholl Brose Cream
Shortbread Biscuits

This Scottish menu begins with oat-crusted trout, followed by a magnificent mutton pie. The dessert is memorable, something you'll want to add to your favourite-recipe list: whisky oranges are topped by a cream adapted from the famous Scottish drink, Atholl Brose. The recipe for this unique whisky-based drink is here for you to try as a liqueur after the meal. A traditional shortbread recipe is also included to serve with coffee. Or, if you want to serve small pieces of the traditional Scottish Black Bun with coffee, we've added this recipe, too. The menu serves 6

Opposite, clockwise from top left: Scottish Mutton Pie, Whisky Oranges with Atholl Brose Cream, Buttered Vegetables, Spinach Dumplings, Golden Oat Trout with Parsley Lemon Butter.

GOLDEN OAT TROUT
6 trout
¾ cup fine oatmeal
1 cup rolled oats
1½ cups fresh breadcrumbs
salt, pepper
flour
2 eggs
¼ cup milk
60g (2oz) butter
3 tablespoons oil

PARSLEY LEMON BUTTER
125g (4oz) butter
1 tablespoon chopped parsley
2 teaspoons lemon juice
1 teaspoon grated lemon rind
salt, pepper

Clean and scale fish. Combine oatmeal, rolled oats, breadcrumbs, salt and pepper. Coat fish with flour, dip in combined beaten eggs and milk, coat well with crumb mixture. Heat butter and oil in large frying pan (or, if using several pans, put the same amount of butter and oil in each pan), fry fish on both sides until golden brown and cooked through. Put on serving plate, top with lemon slices and sliced Parsley Lemon Butter.

Parsley Lemon Butter: Beat butter until light and creamy, fold in parsley, lemon juice, lemon rind, salt and pepper. Spoon mixture in a rough log shape about a quarter of the way down a sheet of greaseproof paper. Fold paper over roll then, with ruler, push against the butter, so the mixture forms a smooth roll. Roll butter in the greaseproof paper, refrigerate until firm; cut into slices.

Note: Fine oatmeal is available in 500g packs at health food stores.

SPINACH DUMPLINGS
500g (1lb) potatoes
315g packet frozen
    chopped spinach
1 egg
½ teaspoon salt
1 cup self-raising flour
60g (2oz) butter
pepper
125g (4oz) bacon
2 tablespoons chopped parsley

Boil peeled and quartered potatoes until tender; drain well. Return potatoes to pan, shake over heat to evaporate any excess moisture. Remove from heat, push potatoes through fine sieve. Place defrosted spinach into pan, stand over medium heat to evaporate all liquid from spinach. Add chopped spinach, lightly beaten egg, salt and sifted flour to potato; mix well. Allow mixture to become cold. With floured hands, take tablespoons of mixture and roll into balls. Drop a quarter of the balls into large pan of simmering water; when they rise to the top of water, simmer 3 minutes. Remove from water with slotted spoon.

Place on absorbent paper. Repeat with remaining spinach balls in batches. Cover with greaseproof paper, leave overnight to dry out. Just before serving, heat butter, pepper and finely-chopped bacon in large frying pan, add dumplings, saute gently for 5 minutes, shaking pan occasionally. Just before serving, add parsley, toss gently.   ▷

BUTTERED VEGETABLES

5 medium carrots
750g (1½lb) peas
2 leeks
60g (2oz) butter
salt, pepper
2 tablespoons water
8 shallots

Place peeled and sliced carrots into pan of boiling salted water, boil uncovered for 3 minutes; drain. Plunge into cold water, leave for 3 minutes; drain. Shell peas, place into boiling salted water, boil uncovered for 3 minutes; drain. Plunge into cold water for 3 minutes; drain. Wash leeks well, cut into thick slices. Heat butter in pan, add leeks, carrots, peas, salt, pepper and the 2 tablespoons water, cook for 2 minutes, then cover, simmer for 5 minutes. Just before serving, add chopped shallots, simmer uncovered for 1 minute.

SCOTTISH MUTTON PIE

FILLING

2kg (4lb) leg mutton (or lamb)
60g (2oz) butter
4 large onions
3 cups water
salt, pepper
¾ cup plain flour
¾ cup water, extra

PASTRY

3 cups plain flour
½ teaspoon salt
125g (4oz) lard
¾ cup water
1 egg yolk
1 tablespoon water, extra

Filling: Lamb can be substituted but mutton gives a much better flavour. Ask butcher to bone out the leg of mutton. Remove all fat and gristle. Cut meat into large cubes. Heat butter in large pan, add half the meat, fry quickly until brown, remove from pan, repeat with remaining meat. Return all meat to pan with peeled and chopped onions, water, salt and pepper. Bring to boil, reduce heat, simmer covered 60 minutes or until meat is tender.

Remove pan from heat. Combine flour and extra water, mix until smooth. Gradually add flour mixture to meat, stir until combined. Return pan to heat, stir until mixture boils and thickens, reduce heat, simmer 5 minutes, stirring occasionally. Allow mixture to become cold. Spoon cold filling into large deep pie dish, approximately 1 litre (4 cup) capacity.

Pastry: Sift flour and salt into bowl. Place lard and water into pan, stand over heat until lard has melted and water comes to boil, remove from heat. Add hot liquid to flour; mix well. Turn on to lightly-floured surface; knead lightly. Cover pastry, stand for 5 minutes. Knead again until smooth. Brush edge of dish with combined egg yolk and extra water. Roll out pastry 5cm (2in.) larger than dish. Cut thin strips from around edge of pastry.

Place strips of pastry around edge of pie dish. Brush strips with egg-yolk mixture. Lift pastry on to dish. Press edges together lightly, trim off excess pastry. Decorate edges. Make a slit in top of pastry. Brush with egg-yolk mixture. Bake in hot oven 10 minutes or until golden brown. Reduce heat to moderate, cook further 60 minutes. If pastry browns too quickly cover with brown paper.

WHISKY ORANGES WITH ATHOLL BROSE CREAM

¾ cup sugar
½ cup water
¼ cup scotch whisky
8 oranges

ATHOLL BROSE CREAM

1½ cups cream
3 tablespoons honey
3 tablespoons scotch whisky

Combine sugar and water in saucepan, stir over heat until sugar dissolves. Bring to boil, reduce heat, simmer 2 minutes. Remove from heat, add whisky, cool. Remove rind from oranges, remove all white pith. Cut oranges into segments, cutting between membranes; do this over bowl, to catch all the juice. Put into bowl, pour cooled syrup over, cover, refrigerate. To serve, spoon oranges and syrup into six individual serving dishes, top with Atholl Brose Cream.

Atholl Brose Cream: Whip cream softly. Put honey and whisky into bowl, stir until well combined. Gradually add whisky mixture to cream, beat until thick. Refrigerate until serving time.

Note: Oranges can be and put into whisky syrup several days in advance to absorb the flavour of the syrup. Put oranges into bowl with syrup, cover tightly, refrigerate.

SHORTBREAD BISCUITS

¾ cup plain flour
2 tablespoons ground rice
125g (4oz) butter
¼ cup sugar
1 egg yolk
1 tablespoon cream

Sift flour and ground rice into bowl, rub in butter until mixture resembles coarse breadcrumbs. Add sugar, combine well. Add combined egg yolk and cream, mix to a firm dough. Cover with plastic food wrap, refrigerate 30 minutes. Roll dough out thinly on lightly-floured board to 3mm (⅛in.) thickness. Cut into rounds with floured 4cm (1½in.) fluted round cutter. Prick top of biscuits with fork, put on greased oven trays, bake in moderately slow oven 15 minutes or until biscuits are very lightly browned. Remove from tray, cool on wire rack. Makes about 35.

ATHOLL BROSE

We give the recipe for this famous drink in two quantities, one using a whole bottle of scotch whisky, the other for just six servings.
½ cup rolled oats
⅔ cup water
4 tablespoons honey
750ml bottle scotch whisky

Put oats and water in bowl, stand 1 hour. Push oat mixture through fine sieve, reserve oat liquid, discard oats. Add honey to oat liquid, mix well. Pour ½ cup whisky out of bottle (reserve this to make Whisky Oranges and Atholl Brose Cream). Pour honey oat mixture into whisky bottle, secure lid, shake bottle to combine. Serve in sherry or liqueur glasses.

Quantities for 6: 1½ cups scotch whisky; ⅓ cup rolled oats; ¼ cup water; 2½ tablespoons honey.

PASTRY
3 cups plain flour
½ teaspoon salt
250g (8oz) butter
1 egg yolk
4 tablespoons water, approximately
1 egg yolk, extra
1 tablespoon water, extra
FILLING
500g (1lb) raisins
125g (4oz) blanched almonds
60g (2oz) mixed peel
500g (1lb) currants
1 teaspoon ground ginger
1 teaspoon cinnamon
1 teaspoon mixed spice
¼ teaspoon finely ground
black pepper
½ cup whisky
½ cup honey
½ cup milk
2 eggs
1½ cups plain flour

STEP 1

Pastry: Sift the flour and salt into a basin, rub in butter; use hand to mix in combined egg yolk and water; you may need to add a teaspoon or two more water but pastry must be very firm. Refrigerate while preparing filling.

Filling: Finely chop the raisins, almonds and peel, combine in basin with currants, spices, pepper, whisky, honey, milk, beaten eggs and sifted flour; mix well with hand or wooden spoon. Roll two-thirds of pastry on floured surface to line base and sides of 23cm x 12cm (9in. x 5in.) loaf tin. Ease pastry down sides of tin and into corners gently with fingers, do not break or stretch. Press out folds in pastry with fingertips; bring pastry above edge of tin, trim with knife or scissors, so pastry is 1cm (½in.) all round above edge of tin. Press filling firmly into pastry case, level top.

STEP 2

Roll remaining pastry about 2.5cm (1in.) larger all round than top of tin, trim with sharp knife to rectangle 1cm (½in.) larger all round than inside measurement of tin. Brush pastry in tin with combined extra egg yolk and extra water, carefully place rectangle of pastry over filling. Pinch edges of pastry together using fingers, as shown. Do not cut slit in top of pastry. Brush surface with egg-yolk mixture. Bake in slow oven 3 to 3½ hours, or until golden brown. Leave to cool in tin until completely cold. Stand tin in hot water for 1 minute, carefully remove bun from tin. □

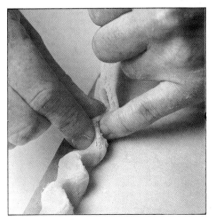

Cream of Chicken Soup with Parsley Dumplings
Wiener Schnitzel
Sauteed Mushrooms
Potato Salad, Green Salad
Apple Strudel

In its cooking, Austria has been influenced by the cuisines of many of the neighbouring countries, but has evolved its own simple and superb way with food. Soup is important, the schnitzels are famous and Austrian pastries are renowned throughout the world. Here is a dinner party menu of Austrian foods which serves 6. Viennese Coffee can be served at the end of the meal — hot, black coffee topped with whipped cream and a sprinkling of cinnamon or nutmeg

Opposite, clockwise from top left: Cream of Chicken Soup with Parsley Dumplings, Potato Salad, Apple Strudel, Wiener Schnitzel and Sauteed Mushrooms, Green Salad.

CREAM OF CHICKEN SOUP
1.25kg (2½lb) chicken
2 litres (8 cups) water
2 large onions
4 sticks celery
90g (3oz) butter
1 medium parsnip
⅓ cup plain flour
salt, pepper
2 chicken stock cubes
½ cup cream

Wash and clean chicken, place into large pan, add water, one peeled and chopped onion and two chopped sticks of celery. Bring to boil, reduce heat, simmer covered for 2 hours. Remove chicken from stock, reserve 7 cups of strained stock or make up to 7 cups with water.

In separate pan, melt butter, add remaining peeled and finely-chopped onion, remaining finely-chopped celery and peeled and finely-chopped parsnip, cook gently until onion is tender. Add flour, stir until combined, cook 1 minute, remove pan from heat. Add reserved stock to pan all at once, stir until combined. Return pan to heat, stir until soup boils and thickens, reduce heat, simmer gently for 2 minutes. Season with salt and pepper, add crumbled stock cubes. Cover pan, simmer gently 10 minutes.

Remove skin from chicken, remove meat from bones. Cut meat into very small pieces. Just before serving, add chicken and cream to pan, heat through gently.

Spoon soup into bowls, or one large serving bowl; top with the hot dumplings. ▷

PARSLEY DUMPLINGS
1 small loaf of white unsliced bread
4 rashers bacon
60g (2oz) butter
30g (1oz) butter, extra
1 medium onion
salt, pepper
2 tablespoons chopped parsley
½ cup plain flour
⅔ cup milk
4 chicken stock cubes

Remove crusts from bread. Cut bread into 1cm (½in.) cubes. You will need 250g (8oz) of bread cubes. Remove rind from bacon, chop bacon finely. Place bacon and butter into frying pan, fry gently until bacon is crisp. Remove bacon from pan, leave fat in pan. Add bread cubes to pan, stir until golden brown, remove from pan. Place extra butter in pan, add peeled and finely-chopped onion, cook gently until onion is light golden brown. Place bread, bacon, onion mixture, salt, pepper, parsley, sifted flour and milk into bowl; mix well. Allow to stand 15 minutes. Take tablespoons of mixture, roll mixture into firm balls. Drop dumplings into large pan of simmering water in which stock cubes have been dissolved. Cover pan, reduce heat, simmer very gently until dumplings have doubled in size, approximately 5 minutes.

WIENER SCHNITZEL
6 veal steaks
flour
2 eggs
3 tablespoons milk
packaged dry breadcrumbs
60g (2oz) butter
2 tablespoons oil
60g (2oz) butter, extra
2 teaspoons lemon juice

Pound veal steaks out thinly, or ask butcher to do this for you. Trim, if necessary, to neat shape. Coat lightly with flour, dip in combined beaten eggs and milk, coat firmly with breadcrumbs. Refrigerate one hour to set the crumbs. Heat butter and oil in pan, cook veal until golden brown on both sides. Remove from pan, drain well. Add extra butter to pan; when melted, add lemon juice. Spoon liquid over steaks.

SAUTEED MUSHROOMS
500g (1lb) small mushrooms
90g (3oz) butter

Trim stalks of mushrooms, cook mushrooms in hot butter until they are golden brown.

POTATO SALAD
1kg (2lb) potatoes
½ cup mayonnaise
½ cup sour cream
2 tablespoons french dressing
2 tablespoons chopped parsley
salt, pepper

Peel potatoes, cut into 2.5cm (1in.) cubes. Cook in boiling salted water until just tender, drain. Combine potatoes with remaining ingredients; serve hot or cold.

PASTRY

1½ cups plain flour
1 egg
1 tablespoon oil
⅓ cup warm water
125g (4oz) butter
60g (2oz) butter, extra

FILLING

4 large apples
½ cup castor sugar
1 teaspoon vanilla
30g (1oz) butter
1 cup fresh white breadcrumbs
½ cup brown sugar, lightly packed
¼ teaspoon nutmeg
1 teaspoon cinnamon
1 teaspoon grated lemon rind
¾ cup sultanas

Filling: Peel and core apples, slice thinly (potato peeler will give very thin slices of apple, which are ideal). Place apple slices into bowl with sugar and vanilla, mix well. Cover bowl, allow to stand 1 hour. Melt 30g (1oz) butter in pan, add breadcrumbs, stir over low heat until breadcrumbs are golden brown; cool. Mix breadcrumbs and brown sugar together. Drain off excess liquid from apples. Combine apples, nutmeg, cinnamon, lemon rind and sultanas in bowl; mix lightly.

STEP 1

Sift flour into bowl, make a well in centre of dry ingredients, add egg and oil. Gradually add water, mixing to a soft dough with hand. Turn out on to lightly-floured surface; knead into a ball. Now pick up dough and throw down on lightly-floured surface; do this about 100 times. Knead again for 5 minutes. The more the dough is banged down and kneaded, the lighter it will be. Form dough into ball and place into lightly-oiled bowl, cover and stand in warm place for 45 minutes. Cover large table with clean cloth, rub flour over surface. Roll out dough as far as it will go.

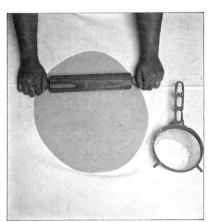

STEP 2

Flour hands, slip them under dough, then start pulling dough from centre with backs of hands, rather than fingers; do this gently and carefully. Continue stretching dough until it is paper-thin and approximately 90cm (36in.) square. Brush with the 125g (4oz) melted butter.

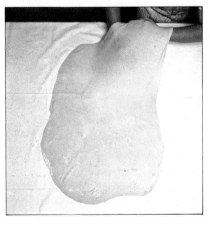

STEP 3

Sprinkle combined breadcrumbs and brown sugar over half the pastry about 5cm (2in.) in from edges. Spoon prepared apple mixture over the breadcrumbs. Fold in sides of pastry over apple filling. Gather cloth in hands and carefully roll up apple strudel, pulling cloth to you as you roll. Place on large greased tray, curving gently and carefully into horseshoe shape. Brush with the 60g (2oz) extra melted butter. Bake in moderately hot oven 35 to 40 minutes. When cold, dust with sifted icing sugar. □

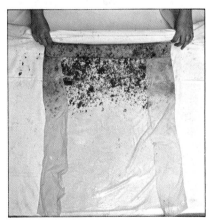

Prawn Cutlets with Crab Sauce Tartare
Chicken with Mushrooms
Broccoli, Saffron Rice
Strawberry Grand Marnier Tarts

This dinner party has many do-ahead features. You'll be able to present three delicious courses to guests with professional ease. What's more, each course is a dish you'll want to make again — soon! This menu serves 6 people

Opposite, clockwise from top left: Prawn Cutlets with Crab and Sauce Tartare, Saffron Rice, Strawberry Grand Marnier Tarts, Chicken with Mushrooms and Broccoli.

CHICKEN WITH MUSHROOMS
6 whole chicken breasts
flour
salt, pepper
125g (4oz) butter
250g (8oz) small mushrooms
2 cloves garlic
1 cup water
1½ cups dry white wine
1 teaspoon french mustard
3 chicken stock cubes
¾ cup sour cream
4 egg yolks
1 teaspoon cornflour
6 shallots

Remove skin from chicken meat. With sharp knife, carefully remove meat from bones, keeping meat in one piece. You will then have 12 pieces of chicken. Pound chicken breasts out lightly. Coat lightly with flour seasoned with salt and pepper. Heat butter in frying pan, add a few pieces of chicken, cook gently until light golden brown; remove from pan, repeat with remaining chicken; remove from pan. Add sliced mushrooms and crushed garlic to pan, cook for 3 minutes. Add water, wine, mustard and crumbled stock cubes, stir until combined. Return chicken to pan, bring to simmering point. Cover pan, simmer gently for 20 minutes. Remove chicken from pan, keep warm. Remove pan from heat, gradually add combined sour cream, egg yolks and cornflour, stir until combined. Season with salt and pepper. Return pan to heat, stir until sauce just comes to simmering point. Simmer very slowly for 2 minutes. Return chicken to pan, simmer further 2 minutes. Add chopped shallots just before serving. ▷

SAFFRON RICE

1 large onion
90g (3oz) butter
½ teaspoon saffron
2 cups long-grain rice
4½ cups water
2 chicken stock cubes
500g packet frozen peas
2 tablespoons chopped parsley

Peel and chop onion, fry in butter until transparent. Add saffron and rice to pan, cook 1 minute, stirring constantly. Add water and crumbled stock cubes, mix well. Bring to boil, reduce heat, simmer covered 15 to 20 minutes or until rice is tender and all water has been absorbed. Add frozen peas 10 minutes before the end of cooking time, stir gently through rice with fork. Stir in parsley.

STRAWBERRY GRAND MARNIER TARTS

PASTRY
1 cup plain flour
pinch salt
2 tablespoons castor sugar
60g (2oz) ground hazelnuts
125g (4oz) butter
1 egg yolk
2 teaspoons water

FILLING
1 tablespoon castor sugar
300ml carton thickened cream
1 tablespoon Grand Marnier
2 punnets strawberries
½ cup strawberry jam
1 tablespoon water
1 tablespoon Grand Marnier, extra

Pastry: Sift flour, salt and sugar into bowl, add hazelnuts; mix well. Rub in butter until mixture resembles coarse breadcrumbs. Add egg yolk and water, mix to a firm dough. Turn out on to lightly-floured surface, knead lightly. Divide dough into 6 equal portions. Roll out each portion to cover base and sides of 6 individual 10cm (4in.) flan tins. Prick pastry well. Place flan tins on to oven trays. Refrigerate for 30 minutes. Cook in moderate oven for 10 to 12 minutes until light golden brown, remove from oven, let cool in tins.

Filling: Place sugar, cream and Grand Marnier into bowl, beat cream until firm peaks form. Spread cream mixture over base of each cold tart. Wash and hull strawberries, cut strawberries in half and arrange over cream. Place strawberry jam, water and extra Grand Marnier into pan, bring to simmering point, remove pan from heat, push through fine sieve. Allow to become cold. Brush jam mixture thickly over strawberries. Refrigerate until ready to serve.

SAUCE TARTARE

¾ cup mayonnaise
2 gherkins
6 shallots
1 tablespoon chopped parsley
1 teaspoon lemon juice
salt, pepper
½ teaspoon dry mustard
½ cup cream

Combine the mayonnaise, finely-chopped gherkins, finely-chopped shallots, parsley, lemon juice, salt, pepper and mustard. Whip cream, fold into mayonnaise mixture. Refrigerate until ready to serve.

Note: This sauce complements the Prawn Cutlets with Crab recipe which follows.

1 kg (2lb) green king prawns
¾ cup plain flour
2 eggs
¼ cup milk
1½ cups packaged dry breadcrumbs
oil for deep frying
FILLING
30g (1oz) butter or substitute
1 tablespoon finely-chopped celery
1 tablespoon finely-chopped
  green pepper
1 clove garlic
1 tablespoon flour
⅓ cup milk
2 x 170g cans crab
½ cup fresh breadcrumbs
½ teaspoon worcestershire sauce
½ teaspoon lemon juice
1 teaspoon salt

Filling: Melt butter in pan, add celery, pepper and crushed garlic, cook 2 minutes until vegetables are tender. Add flour, stir until smooth, cook 1 minute. Remove from heat, add milk, stir until smooth. Return to heat, stir until sauce boils and thickens, reduce heat, simmer 30 seconds. Remove from heat, add drained flaked crab, breadcrumbs, worcestershire sauce, lemon juice and salt, mix well.

STEP 1

Shell prawns, leaving tail intact. Using a sharp knife, make a slit down back of prawns, remove back veins.

STEP 2

Now cut a deeper slit down back of each prawn, taking care not to cut through flesh completely.

STEP 3

Put approximately 1 tablespoon of filling into each slit, reshape prawn. Refrigerate 1 hour.

STEP 4

Roll prawns in flour, shake off excess. Dip in combined beaten eggs and milk, toss in breadcrumbs. Dip in the egg mixture again, toss in breadcrumbs again.

(Prawns can be returned to refrigerator at this stage until required.) Deep-fry prawns in hot oil, a few at a time, for three minutes or until golden brown and crisp, drain. Serve prawns with Sauce Tartare. ☐

Individual Camembert and Crab Quiches
Roast Turkey with Pine Nut Stuffing
Brown Rice, Green Beans
Cointreau Ice-cream with Chocolate Oranges

Turkey — the noble bird — is too good to keep for Christmas alone. Here we fill it with a mushroom and pine nut stuffing, and serve it with a port-flavoured sauce. For starters, delicious quiches made in individual servings — and for dessert, fresh-tasting home-made ice-cream, flavoured with liqueur. The menu serves 6

Opposite, from front: Roast Turkey with Pine Nut Stuffing, Brown Rice and Green Beans, Individual Camembert and Crab Quiches, and Cointreau Ice-cream with Chocolate Oranges.

ROAST TURKEY WITH PINE NUT STUFFING

3kg (6lb) turkey
45g (1½oz) butter
salt, pepper
1 cup water
2 tablespoons flour
½ cup port
½ cup water, extra
1 chicken stock cube
STUFFING
90g (3oz) butter
50g packet pine nuts
1 onion
2 rashers bacon
125g (4oz) mushrooms
3 cups fresh breadcrumbs
　(approx ½ loaf)
1 egg

Fill turkey with prepared stuffing; tie legs together to keep in good shape. Rub softened butter well into the bird, particularly over breast and legs. Sprinkle lightly with salt and pepper. Cover with well-buttered aluminium foil. Place in baking dish, pour 1 cup water into dish. Cook in moderate oven, basting frequently. Remove foil halfway through cooking to allow bird to brown. Allow approximately 3 hours cooking time. To test if bird is cooked, put a skewer into the thick section of leg; juices should run clear, not pink. When turkey is cooked and golden brown, transfer to heated serving dish. Add flour to juices in baking dish, let mixture cook 1 minute. Stir in port, extra water and crumbled stock cube, mix well, stir until boiling, reduce heat, simmer 3 minutes; season with salt and pepper.

Stuffing: Melt butter in pan, add pine nuts, peeled and finely-chopped onion; remove rind from bacon, chop bacon finely, add to pan with finely-chopped mushrooms. Cook until onion is transparent, remove from heat, add remaining ingredients, mix well. ▷

BROWN RICE
water
2 cups brown rice
30g (1oz) butter
125g (4oz) slivered almonds
1 tablespoon oil

Bring a large saucepan of water to the boil, add rice gradually; boil uncovered for 30 minutes or until rice is tender, drain. Melt butter in pan, add almonds, stir over heat until almonds are golden brown, drain on absorbent paper. Just before serving, heat oil in pan, add rice and almonds, toss until combined and heated through.

COINTREAU ICE-CREAM WITH CHOCOLATE ORANGES
ICE-CREAM
5 eggs
½ cup sugar
300ml carton cream
¼ cup sugar, extra
2 tablespoons Cointreau
CHOCOLATE ORANGES
1 large firm orange
125g (4oz) dark chocolate

Ice-cream: Put eggs and the ½ cup sugar in top of double saucepan. Beat over hot water until the sugar dissolves and the mixture is lukewarm. Remove from heat, beat until thick and creamy. Whip cream and extra sugar until firm. Fold egg mixture and Cointreau into cream, mix well. Spoon mixture into freezer tray. Cover with aluminium foil, freeze until firm, stirring occasionally. Decorate with Chocolate Oranges.

Chocolate Oranges: Peel orange carefully, removing all white pith; divide into segments. Melt chopped chocolate in top of double saucepan, place orange segments one at a time into chocolate, coat with chocolate, lift out with fork, drain; place on aluminium foil. Refrigerate.

TO SERVE WITH COFFEE
These easy-to-make biscuits are perfect mouthfuls to serve your guests with their after-dinner coffee.

FLORENTINES
1 cup cornflakes
30g (1oz) red glace cherries
½ cup sultanas
½ cup raw peanuts
⅓ cup condensed milk
60g (2oz) dark chocolate

Combine in a bowl slightly-crushed cornflakes, finely-chopped cherries, sultanas, peanuts and condensed milk, mix well. Line oven trays with greased greaseproof paper, dust lightly with flour. Drop teaspoonfuls on to oven trays. Bake in moderate oven 8 minutes or until edges begin to turn brown. Leave on trays to cool. Use a spatula to remove when cold. Melt chopped chocolate in top of double saucepan over simmering water. Using a spatula, spread chocolate on base of cooled biscuit. Mark wavy lines on chocolate with a fork. Let chocolate set. Makes 24.

PASTRY
2 cups plain flour
¼ teaspoon baking powder
pinch salt
150g (5oz) butter
1 egg yolk
1 teaspoon lemon juice
1 tablespoon water
FILLING
150g can camembert cheese
155g can crab
4 shallots
4 eggs
¾ cup cream
2 tablespoons sour cream
salt, pepper

STEP 1

Pastry: Sift dry ingredients into bowl, rub in butter until mixture resembles dry breadcrumbs. Mix to a firm dough with lightly-beaten egg yolk, lemon juice and water. Turn pastry on to lightly-floured surface, knead lightly. Divide into 6 equal portions. Roll each portion out thinly to fit base and sides of six 10cm (4in.) flan tins.

STEP 2

Fit pastry neatly into tins. Roll rolling pin over top of each tin quickly and firmly; this will cut off excess pastry and leave a neat clean edge. Refrigerate until ready to use.

STEP 3

Filling: Slice cheese thinly. Sprinkle drained flaked crab over base of each individual quiche, top with sliced cheese. Sprinkle the finely-chopped shallots over top of cheese.

STEP 4

Beat eggs together lightly, combine with cream, sour cream, salt and pepper. Pour carefully into each individual quiche. Bake in moderately hot oven 10 minutes, reduce heat to moderate, cook further 15 to 20 minutes or until filling is set. □

Asparagus with Minted Hollandaise Sauce
Braised Chicken with Vegetables Julienne
Buttered New Potatoes
Creamed Spinach
Creme Caramel with Toffee Strawberries

This dinner party is light and beautifully flavoured — tender young asparagus for entree, succulent chicken with vegetables for main course, and a superb creme caramel with toffee strawberries for dessert. A board of fresh, crusty breads and rolls adds interest to the table. This menu serves 6

Opposite, clockwise from top left: Buttered New Potatoes and Creamed Spinach, Braised Chicken with Vegetables Julienne, Asparagus with Minted Hollandaise Sauce, and Creme Caramel with Toffee Strawberries.

ASPARAGUS WITH MINTED HOLLANDAISE SAUCE
2 bunches fresh asparagus
HOLLANDAISE SAUCE
3 tablespoons white vinegar
1 bayleaf
6 peppercorns
125g (4oz) butter
2 egg yolks
salt, pepper
2 teaspoons lemon juice
¼ cup chopped mint

Cut off tough ends of asparagus, scrape spears a few centimetres up from end, tie in a bunch. Stand in a deep, tall saucepan and add boiling salted water to come halfway up spears. Cover tightly, bring to boil, reduce heat and simmer until asparagus is tender (approximately 20 minutes, although very young asparagus will take only 10 to 15 minutes). Drain well. Asparagus can also be cooked in a covered shallow pan of boiling water for approximately 15 minutes although the tender tips of the asparagus tend to cook more quickly than the stems.

Hollandaise Sauce: Simmer vinegar, bayleaf and peppercorns gently together, uncovered, until liquid is reduced to half quantity; strain, reserve liquid. Work butter until slightly soft. Cream egg yolks with a little of the butter and salt in top of double saucepan; stir in strained liquid. Stir over very low heat until just beginning to thicken. Add remaining butter in small pieces, stirring continually, and frequently removing saucepan from heat while you stir. When all butter has been added, add pepper and lemon juice. When ready to serve, stir in the mint. To serve, arrange asparagus on a plate, spoon sauce over. ▷

BRAISED CHICKEN WITH VEGETABLES JULIENNE

3 x 1kg (2lb) chickens
90g (3oz) butter
1 tablespoon oil
2 cloves garlic
1½ tablespoons flour
1¾ cups water
2 chicken stock cubes
¼ cup port
¼ cup brandy
1 teaspoon thyme
2 teaspoons soy sauce
pepper
3 small carrots
3 sticks celery

Cut chickens in half lengthways. Heat butter and oil in baking tray, add crushed garlic and chicken halves, cut side down. Bake in moderately hot oven 30 to 35 minutes or until golden brown, basting chicken frequently with pan juices. Remove chicken from pan, pour off excess fat, leaving ⅓ cup fat in pan. Add flour, cook until dark golden brown, stirring constantly; add water, crumbled stock cubes, port, brandy, thyme, soy sauce and pepper; cook, stirring until sauce boils and thickens. Return chicken to pan, cut side down, bake covered in moderate oven 25 to 30 minutes or until chicken is tender, spooning sauce frequently over chicken. Cut carrots and celery into thin strips, 5cm x 2mm (2in. x 1/16in.), add to chicken, mix well. Bake covered in moderate oven further 10 to 15 minutes or until vegetables are tender.

BUTTERED NEW POTATOES

1kg (2lb) small new potatoes
125g (4oz) butter
salt, pepper
2 tablespoons chopped parsley

Peel potatoes, put in boiling salted water, cook approximately 15 minutes or until potatoes are tender; drain well. Heat butter in pan, add salt, pepper, parsley and potatoes, toss until well combined.

Note: Potatoes can be peeled either before or after cooking.

CREAMED SPINACH

1 large bunch spinach
60g (2oz) butter
1 onion
1 clove garlic
salt, pepper
½ cup sour cream
4 shallots
pinch nutmeg

Wash spinach, remove white stems, chop leaves roughly. Put spinach in pan with approximately ¼ cup hot water. Cover tightly, cook until tender, approximately 5 minutes. Drain, pressing out all moisture. Heat butter in pan, add peeled and chopped onion and crushed garlic, cook until onion is tender. Add spinach, salt, pepper and nutmeg, stir until spinach is heated through. Add sour cream and chopped shallots, cook further 3 minutes.

CARAMEL
¾ **cup sugar**
1 cup water
CUSTARD
2 cups milk
300ml carton cream
4 eggs
½ **cup castor sugar**
1 teaspoon vanilla
3 egg yolks, extra
300ml carton cream, extra
TOFFEE STRAWBERRIES
1 punnet strawberries
2 cups sugar
1 cup water

STEP 1

Caramel: Place sugar and water in medium-sized saucepan, stir over low heat until sugar dissolves, brushing down sides of saucepan with a brush dipped in hot water to dissolve any sugar grains. Stop stirring, increase heat, bring to boil, boil until mixture turns deep golden brown; do not stir.

STEP 2

Pour caramel evenly into six individual souffle dishes (caramel will set almost immediately, like toffee). Work quickly; rotate dishes so that caramel coats base and sides of dishes. Use a cloth to protect hands; dishes become hot quickly.

STEP 3

Custard: Place eggs, extra yolks, vanilla and sugar in bowl, beat lightly to combine. Combine milk and cream in saucepan, bring to scalding point (when small bubbles appear on surface), cool slightly. Pour over egg mixture, stirring all the time, strain into jug to remove any small specks of egg and ensure velvety texture. Put caramel-lined dishes into shallow baking dish containing approximately 2cm (¾in.) cold water. Pour custard mixture evenly into each dish.

STEP 4

Bake in moderately slow oven for approximately 30 to 35 minutes or until custard is set. Remove dishes from water, cool. Cover each dish with aluminium foil, refrigerate several hours or overnight. To serve, ease custards away from sides of dishes

with fingers. Turn out on to individual serving plates, decorate with a swirl of extra whipped cream and Toffee Strawberries.

Toffee Strawberries: Wash the strawberries gently, spread on absorbent paper to dry. Put sugar and water in small saucepan, stir over low heat until sugar has dissolved. Increase heat and bring to boil. Boil syrup until it becomes very pale gold in colour. Remove from heat immediately. Using tongs, dip strawberries by stems into the syrup, coating the entire fruit except the stems. Put on lightly-greased baking trays and leave until toffee has hardened. Serve within an hour. If kept too long, the strawberry juice will make toffee sticky. □

Prosciutto and Melon
Veal with Crab
Potato and Onion Casserole
Avocado and Bacon Salad
Black Forest Ice-cream

A dinner party designed to give superb results with the minimum of fuss. The recipes are so quick and easy — perfect for women who have busy lifestyles. This menu serves 6

Opposite, clockwise from top: Prosciutto and Melon, Potato and Onion Casserole, Avocado and Bacon Salad, Veal with Crab, and Black Forest Ice-cream.

PROSCIUTTO AND MELON
1 lettuce
2 melons (rockmelon or honeydew)
1 lemon
6 slices prosciutto
12 black olives

Wash lettuce, dry thoroughly. Cut melons into quarters, remove seeds; cut lemon into 6 wedges. Put a lettuce leaf on each of 6 individual serving dishes, place melon wedge on top. Put 1 slice of prosciutto over each melon wedge, garnish with the olives and lemon wedges.

Note: Prosciutto is Italian raw ham, available at most large food stores. If unobtainable, you can substitute thin slices of leg ham. ▷

VEAL WITH CRAB

6 veal steaks
flour
salt, pepper
3 eggs
packaged dry breadcrumbs
90g (3oz) butter
155g can crab
3 shallots
SAUCE
60g (2oz) butter
3 shallots
60g (2oz) mushrooms
2 teaspoons cornflour
¾ cup water
1 chicken stock cube
¼ cup dry white wine
2 egg yolks
⅔ cup cream
2 tablespoons mayonnaise
1½ teaspoons french mustard
salt, pepper

Pound out veal steaks thinly. Coat veal in flour seasoned with salt and pepper. Dip into beaten eggs, then coat veal in dry breadcrumbs. Heat butter in pan, add veal, cook on both sides until golden brown and cooked through, approximately 8 to 10 minutes. Remove from pan, keep warm while making sauce. To serve, put veal on serving dish, spoon sauce over, top with drained, lightly-flaked crab and chopped shallots.

Sauce: Heat butter in pan, then add chopped shallots and sliced mushrooms, cook until mushrooms are just tender. Blend cornflour with water, add to pan with crumbled stock cube and wine, stir until sauce boils and thickens. Reduce heat, simmer uncovered 2 minutes. Combine lightly-beaten egg yolks, cream, mayonnaise, mustard, salt and pepper in bowl; mix well. Add cream mixture to pan, whisking well until sauce thickens. Do not allow to boil.

POTATO AND ONION CASSEROLE

1kg (2lb) potatoes
salt, pepper
2 large onions
300ml carton cream

Peel potatoes and slice thinly. Put a layer of potato in base of greased ovenproof dish, sprinkle with salt and pepper. Peel onions, slice thinly, arrange a layer of onions over potato slices. Put cream in saucepan, stir over medium heat until cream is heated through. Spoon approximately ¼ cup cream over onion slices. Continue in layers of potato, salt, pepper, onion and cream, finishing with a potato layer. Bake, covered, in moderate oven 30 minutes. Remove the cover, cook for a further 45 minutes or until the potatoes are tender and golden brown.

AVOCADO AND BACON SALAD

1 lettuce
3 medium tomatoes
1 avocado
bottled french dressing
2 rashers bacon
1 tablespoon chopped parsley

Wash lettuce, dry thoroughly; put in plastic bag in refrigerator to crisp. Cut tomatoes into quarters. Peel avocado, cut in half and remove seed; slice avocado thinly, dip in french dressing to prevent discoloration. Chop bacon finely, fry until crisp, drain on absorbent paper. At serving time, tear lettuce into pieces, place on individual serving dishes, add tomatoes and avocado, sprinkle with french dressing, top with bacon and parsley.

2 litre carton vanilla ice-cream
250g (8oz) dark chocolate
30g (1oz) solid white vegetable
  shortening
2 x 425g cans black cherries
2 tablespoons Cherry Heering,
  maraschino or rum
2 tablespoons cornflour
2 tablespoons water

STEP 1

Put an oven tray into freezer so that it is very cold. Remove ice-cream container from freezer. Dip ice-cream scoop into cold water, scoop ice-cream into balls with ice-cream scoop; place immediately on tray in freezer. Dip ice-cream scoop into cold water again. Repeat with remaining ice-cream to give six ice-cream balls. Freeze until very hard.

STEP 2

Put chopped chocolate and white vegetable shortening into top of double saucepan, stand over hot water; stir until melted, cool. Cover an oven tray with aluminium foil. Dip the ice-cream balls in chocolate, lift out with fork, place on foil-covered trays. Work quickly when doing this. Return ice-cream balls to freezer.

STEP 4

Add pitted cherries to sauce mixture, stir over heat until heated through. Place ice-cream balls in serving dishes, top with the hot cherry sauce, serve immediately.   □

STEP 3

Drain cherries, reserve 1½ cups of syrup. Put reserved cherry syrup and Cherry Heering or maraschino or rum in pan; add combined cornflour and water. Stir until mixture boils and thickens.

Prawn and Haddock Pate Melba Toast
Lemon-Garlic Racks of Lamb
Minted Wine Jelly, Green Peas
Hashed Brown Potatoes
Strawberry Shortcake

In this elegant dinner party menu the pate for the first course can be made the day before; the wine jelly can be made one or two days before; the base for the strawberry shortcake can be cooked the day before — then decorated and glazed on the day of serving. Menu serves 6

Opposite, clockwise from top left: Strawberry Shortcake, Hashed Brown Potatoes, Lemon-Garlic Racks of Lamb, Prawn and Haddock Pate with Melba Toast, Minted Wine Jelly.

PRAWN AND HADDOCK PATE
250g (8oz) small prawns
375g (12oz) haddock
60g (2oz) butter
3 tablespoons plain flour
1 cup milk
½ cup sour cream
½ teaspoon french mustard
salt, pepper
2 teaspoons gelatine
¼ cup water
½ cup mayonnaise
1 tablespoon lemon juice
2 egg whites
chopped parsley

Shell prawns, reserve 12 for garnish. Place haddock into pan, cover with water. Bring to boil, reduce heat, simmer covered for 5 minutes or until haddock is cooked; drain, cool. Heat butter in pan, add flour, stir until combined. Add milk and the sour cream, stir until combined. Stir until the sauce boils and thickens, add mustard, salt and pepper. Reduce heat, simmer sauce for 3 minutes.

Flake haddock, remove all bones. Place white sauce and haddock into electric blender. Blend on medium speed 1 minute or until mixture is smooth. Sprinkle gelatine over water, dissolve over hot water. Add gelatine mixture to haddock mixture, stir until combined, allow mixture to cool to warm. Add mayonnaise, prawns and lemon juice, stir until combined. Beat egg whites until firm peaks form, gently fold into haddock mixture. Pour mixture into 6 individual bowls, cover and refrigerate several hours. To serve, sprinkle with a little chopped parsley, top each bowl with 2 prawns. Serve with Melba Toast. ▷

LEMON-GARLIC RACKS OF LAMB

6 racks of lamb (see below)
2 cups dry white wine
2 cloves garlic
2 tablespoons sugar
¼ cup lemon juice
½ teaspoon rosemary
60g (2oz) butter
3 cups soft white breadcrumbs
90g (3oz) butter, extra
salt, pepper
1 egg
4 tablespoons plain flour
3 cups water
3 chicken stock cubes
2 tablespoons sweet sherry

Ask butcher to cut six individual racks of lamb. Small baby lamb is best for these racks as the chops are small, sweet and tender. Depending on size of cutlets, the racks should contain four to six cutlets. Ask butcher to trim the bones well to give a neat shape. (It is best to order these in advance.)

Trim any surplus fat from cutlets. Place wine, crushed garlic, sugar, lemon juice and rosemary into large bowl, add racks of lamb. Spoon marinade over lamb. Cover bowl and refrigerate for several hours or overnight; spoon marinade over lamb frequently.

Remove lamb from marinade, place into large baking dish, skin side up. Dot each with butter, pour 1 cup of marinade over; reserve remainder of marinade for sauce. Cook in moderate oven 25 minutes, remove from oven. Place breadcrumbs, extra melted butter, salt and pepper into bowl; mix well. Add egg, mix well. Press breadcrumb mixture over skin side of lamb, pressing on firmly. Return lamb to oven for a further 40 minutes or until lamb is tender and breadcrumbs are golden brown. Remove lamb from baking dish; keep warm.

Place baking dish on top of stove, stand over high heat until all liquid has evaporated, pour off excess fat from the pan, leaving approximately 4 tablespoons of fat. Add flour, stir until dark golden brown, remove dish from heat. Add water, crumbled stock cubes, sherry and 1 cup of the reserved marinade, stir until combined. Return pan to heat, stir until sauce boils and thickens, stirring well on base of dish to take up all pan drippings. Season with salt and pepper. Reduce heat, simmer sauce uncovered for 5 minutes, stirring occasionally.

MINTED WINE JELLY

2 cups dry white wine
½ cup water
5cm (2in.) piece orange rind
2 large sprigs mint
½ cup white vinegar
½ cup sugar
1 tablespoon gelatine
3 tablespoons chopped mint
1 tablespoon chopped chives

Place wine, water, orange rind, sprigs of mint and vinegar into saucepan. Bring to boil, reduce heat, simmer uncovered for 5 minutes. Remove sprigs of mint and allow to cool slightly. Add sugar, stir until sugar is dissolved. Sprinkle gelatine over wine mixture, stir until gelatine is dissolved. Add chopped mint, stir until combined. Cover bowl, place into refrigerator until mixture is the consistency of unbeaten egg white. Stir mixture occasionally so that mint will be evenly distributed through jelly. When set, spoon into serving bowl, top with chopped chives, keep refrigerated until ready to serve.

HASHED BROWN POTATOES

1.5kg (3lb) old potatoes
60g (2oz) butter
2 rashers bacon

Peel and quarter potatoes, boil until tender. Drain, allow to become cold. Place butter and finely-chopped bacon into very large frying pan. Saute until bacon is very crisp. Remove bacon from pan, keep all fat in pan. Spread roughly-mashed potatoes into pan, pressing down evenly and firmly. Fry potatoes over the lowest heat for approximately 30 minutes, so that base of potatoes is dark golden brown. To serve, place potatoes into hot serving bowl; use spatula to take up all of the brown crisp potato. Sprinkle bacon over.

STRAWBERRY SHORTCAKE

60g (2oz) butter
2 tablespoons sugar
2 egg yolks
¾ cup plain flour
1 punnet strawberries
½ cup strawberry jam
2 teaspoons water

Cream butter and sugar until light and fluffy, add egg yolks, beat well. Work in sifted flour until well combined, knead dough on lightly-floured board. Press dough into lightly-greased 20cm (8in.) sandwich tin, bake in moderate oven 15 to 20 minutes. Remove from tin, allow to cool slightly.

Reserve a few strawberries for decoration. Hull the remaining strawberries, cut in halves, arrange over warm shortcake.

Combine jam and water, stir over low heat until boiling, push through sieve. Cool slightly, then brush generously over strawberries and shortcake. Refrigerate until set. Decorate with whipped cream and reserved strawberries; brush some of the jam glaze over the reserved strawberries for a pretty effect.

STEP 1

Take a square loaf of unsliced bread, remove all crusts. Cut bread in half, giving two half loaves (this way it is easier to handle the cutting of individual slices).

STEP 2

Now cut each loaf diagonally in half, giving four thick triangle-shaped bread pieces.

STEP 3

Place flat side on board, as shown. Cut into wafer-thin slices. An electric knife is good for this, but any serrated or sharp knife can be used. Place triangles on ungreased baking trays. Bake in moderate oven 15 to 20 minutes, or until light golden brown, turning frequently. Melba Toast will keep well for about two weeks if stored in an airtight container. □

Minted Carrot Soup
Spinach Quiche
Hot Tomato Salad
Green Salad
Apricot Yoghurt Slice

The tempting recipes in this vegetarian dinner party serve 6. For drink accompaniments, choose from non-alcoholic sparkling grape drinks or tingling apple cider

Opposite, clockwise from top left: Spinach Quiche, Hot Tomato Salad, Green Salad, Minted Carrot Soup, and Apricot Yoghurt Slice.

MINTED CARROT SOUP

1 kg (2lb) carrots
1 onion
2 potatoes
2 sticks celery
6 shallots
90g (3oz) butter
1 clove garlic
1 litre (4 cups) water
2 teaspoons sugar
salt
2 tablespoons chopped parsley
2 teaspoons chopped mint
½ cup cream

Peel and slice carrots, onion and potatoes. Wash and chop celery and shallots. Melt butter in large saucepan, add carrots, crushed garlic, potatoes, onion, celery and shallots, stir to coat vegetables in butter. Cover pan, cook gently approximately 5 minutes, stirring occasionally; do not let the vegetables brown. Add water, sugar and salt. Simmer gently, covered, approximately 10 minutes until vegetables are tender. Stir in chopped parsley and mint. Blend vegetables and liquid until smooth in electric blender. Blend only one cup of soup at a time. Return soup to saucepan, stir in cream, reheat without boiling. ▷

SPINACH QUICHE

PASTRY
½ cup wholemeal self-raising flour
½ cup wholemeal plain flour
½ teaspoon salt
125g (4oz) butter
2 teaspoons lemon juice
1 egg yolk

FILLING
250g (8oz) packet frozen
   chopped spinach
2 tablespoons oil
½ cup chopped shallots
¼ cup chopped parsley
1 clove garlic
¼ teaspoon dill
125g (4oz) cottage cheese
125g (4oz) feta cheese
2 eggs

Pastry: Sift flours and salt into basin, return husks from sifter to basin. Rub in butter, add lemon juice and egg yolk, mix to a pliable dough with hand. Turn on to lightly-floured surface, roll out to line 23cm (9in.) flan tin, trim edges. Bake in moderately hot oven 10 to 15 minutes, or until light golden brown; cool. Spread evenly with cold filling, bake in moderate oven 20 to 30 minutes, or until set.

Filling: Put spinach in basin, allow to thaw, reserve liquid. Heat oil in pan, add shallots, parsley and crushed garlic, cook until tender, add spinach and liquid, and dill. Stir constantly over heat for two minutes, remove from heat; cool. When cold, stir in the sieved cheeses and lightly-beaten eggs; mix well.

HOT TOMATO SALAD

500g (1lb) tomatoes
2 onions
1 tablespoon oil
1 tablespoon chopped fresh basil
   (or ½ teaspoon dry basil)
3 shallots
salt

Peel tomatoes, chop roughly; peel and chop onions. Heat oil in pan, add onions, cook until the onions are transparent. Add tomatoes, stir over medium heat until tomatoes are heated through. Remove from heat, stir in basil and chopped shallots. Season with salt.

APRICOT YOGHURT SLICE

BASE
¼ cup toasted coconut (see below)
125g (4oz) Granita biscuits
60g (2oz) butter

FILLING
125g (4oz) dried apricots
½ cup boiling water
2 x 200g cartons plain yoghurt
3 tablespoons honey
2 eggs

Base: To toast coconut, place coconut in heavy pan, stir with wooden spoon over moderate heat until coconut is light golden brown, remove from pan immediately. Combine in bowl finely-crushed biscuits, toasted coconut and melted butter, mix well. Line 18cm x 28cm (7in. x 11in.) lamington tin with aluminium foil. Press crumb mixture evenly over base of tin, refrigerate while preparing filling.

Filling: Cover apricots with boiling water, stand 30 minutes, put apricots and liquid in blender, blend until smooth. Add yoghurt, honey and eggs, blend until smooth. Spread yoghurt mixture over base, bake in moderate oven 30 to 35 minutes or until set. Cool, then refrigerate several hours before serving. Sprinkle top with a little extra toasted coconut.

1 egg white
⅓ cup icing sugar
½ teaspoon vanilla
30g (1oz) butter
30g (1oz) ground almonds
¼ cup plain flour
30g (1oz) dark chocolate
1 teaspoon solid white
   vegetable shortening
whipped cream

STEP 1

Beat egg white with fork until foamy, beat in sifted icing sugar and vanilla, then melted butter and almonds, mix lightly. Fold in sifted flour. Lightly grease two oven trays, mark 8cm (3in.) circles on trays using plain cutter. Mark only two circles on each tray.

STEP 2

Drop teaspoonfuls of mixture into circles, spread to fill circle. Bake in moderately hot oven 5 to 6 minutes. Cornets are ready when mixture is very light golden brown around edges. Only bake two cornets at a time as they have to be shaped very quickly.

STEP 3

Lift cornets quickly from trays, roll into cone shape, hold lightly with fingers until crisp; this takes only a few seconds. Continue cooking until mixture is used.

STEP 4

Melt chocolate and vegetable shortening in top of double saucepan over hot water. Remove from heat, cool; dip open ends of cornets into melted chocolate. Allow chocolate to set. Fill with whipped cream just before serving.

Note: Cornets should be made on the day they are to be served. □

Souffle Oysters
Camembert Chicken
New Potatoes
Green Salad with
Avocado Dressing
Strawberry Hazelnut Slice

There is something delightfully different in each course of this dinner party. And although it presents superb food, the cost is not expensive. These delicious dishes serve 6

Opposite: Camembert Chicken with New Potatoes.

SOUFFLE OYSTERS
24 oysters on the shell
3 rashers bacon
60g (2oz) butter
1½ tablespoons plain flour
½ cup milk
1 teaspoon french mustard
salt, pepper
60g (2oz) cheddar cheese
2 eggs, separated

Put oysters on to baking tray. Remove rind from bacon, chop bacon into small pieces. Put into frying pan, cook until bacon is crisp; sprinkle evenly over oysters. Heat butter in saucepan, add flour, stir until combined, remove from heat. Gradually add milk, stir until combined. Add mustard, salt and pepper. Return pan to heat, stir until sauce boils and thickens, remove from heat. Add grated cheese, stir until cheese has melted. Add egg yolks, stir until combined. Allow mixture to cool until warm. Beat egg whites until soft peaks form, gently fold into cheese mixture. Spoon heaped teaspoonfuls of mixture on to each oyster. Bake in hot oven 5 minutes or until puffed and golden brown. Serve immediately. Allow 4 oysters per serving.

CAMEMBERT CHICKEN
3 x 1kg (2lb) chickens
2 cloves garlic
45g (1½oz) butter
2 x 125g packets camembert cheese
125g (4oz) butter, extra
4 cups fresh white breadcrumbs
60g (2oz) blanched almonds
salt, pepper

Rub chicken skins with cut cloves of garlic. Cut 45g (1½oz) butter into small pieces, put some pieces of butter under skin of each chicken breast. Cut camembert cheeses into nine pieces; put three pieces in each chicken cavity. Put chickens into baking dish, brush over 30g (1oz) of the extra melted butter. Bake in moderate oven 30 minutes, basting frequently. Melt remaining 90g (3oz) butter in pan, add breadcrumbs and finely-chopped almonds, toss gently in butter until all butter has been absorbed. Season with salt and pepper. Remove chickens from oven. Carefully remove cheese from cavity and spread over chickens. Then pack breadcrumbs firmly on to each chicken. Return chickens to oven for a further 1 hour or until golden brown and tender. Cut chickens in half lengthways; allow one half per serving. Serve with new potatoes: when cooked, drain, return to saucepan, toss in butter and chopped parsley. ▷

GREEN SALAD WITH AVOCADO DRESSING

1 lettuce
6 shallots

DRESSING
1 avocado
¼ cup bottled french dressing
¼ cup water
salt, pepper

Wash lettuce, tear into large pieces, toss in bowl with chopped shallots. Peel avocado, chop roughly and put in blender with dressing, water, salt and pepper, blend on high speed until smooth (if dressing is still too thick add a little extra water).

Other greens — such as endive or watercress — can be added to the lettuce for a contrast of colour and flavour. Serve dressing separately for guests to help themselves.

STRAWBERRY HAZELNUT SLICE

3 eggs, separated
½ cup castor sugar
1 cup self-raising flour
3 tablespoons ground hazelnuts
3 tablespoons hot water
1 teaspoon butter
2 tablespoons Cointreau or Grand Marnier
2 teaspoons milk
extra icing sugar
1 tablespoon strawberry jam
1 teaspoon water

FILLING
1 punnet strawberries
½ cup icing sugar
3 teaspoons gelatine
1½ tablespoons water
300ml carton cream

Beat egg whites until soft peaks form, gradually add sugar, beating well after each addition. Add yolks, all at once, beat only until colour is evenly mixed through. Sift flour several times, then sift flour and hazelnuts over egg mixture and fold through lightly (return any remaining hazelnuts in sifter to bowl). Combine hot water and butter, stir until butter melts, pour all at once over mixture, fold through quickly. Pour into greased and greased greaseproof/paper lined 28cm x 18cm (11in. x 7in.) lamington tin. Bake in moderate oven 20 to 25 minutes or until lightly browned and elastic to touch. Turn immediately on to wire rack, cool.

Using a sharp knife, cut cake in half horizontally. Line 28cm x 18cm (11in. x 7in.) lamington tin with aluminium foil. Place bottom half of cake in tin, sprinkle combined Cointreau and milk over cake. Spread prepared filling over cake, place remaining half of cake on top. Refrigerate until filling has set.

To serve, remove slice from refrigerator, remove from tin, trim edges, dust top with extra sifted icing sugar. Heat jam and water in small saucepan, push through sieve. Cut reserved strawberries in half, brush with the glaze, decorate top of slice.

Filling: Reserve 3 strawberries for decoration. Wash and hull remaining strawberries, place in blender, blend on high speed 30 seconds. Add icing sugar, blend further 30 seconds. Sprinkle gelatine over water, stand over hot water until gelatine has dissolved, cool slightly. Whip cream until soft peaks form, stir in strawberry mixture, quickly fold in dissolved gelatine.

Here's a sweet treat to serve with after-dinner coffee. This recipe — using only one egg white — makes abut 90 little just-a-mouthful biscuits; when joined together with the coffee cream, there are about 45 complete biscuits. If you do not want to bother piping all these small meringues, pipe just the amount required then pipe the remaining mixture into larger meringues for later use; keep the meringues in airtight container.

¾ cup raw sugar
1 teaspoon instant coffee powder
2 tablespoons water
1 egg white
1 teaspoon vinegar
2 teaspoons cornflour

COFFEE CREAM
60g (2oz) butter
⅔ cup icing sugar
1 teaspoon instant coffee powder
2 teaspoons hot water
2 teaspoons coffee liqueur
   (Tia Maria or Kahlua)

STEP 1

Combine sugar, coffee and water in saucepan, stir constantly over low heat until sugar is dissolved (this will take about 5 minutes, as raw sugar is more difficult to dissolve than white sugar). It may be necessary to brush sides of saucepan with brush dipped in water to make sure all grains are dissolved. Increase heat, bring to boil, remove from heat immediately. Combine egg white, vinegar and cornflour in small basin of electric mixer, beat until foamy; keep mixer going on medium speed and pour hot coffee syrup in a constant thin stream on to egg white, then beat 10 minutes or until thick. Lightly grease two oven trays, dust with cornflour, shake off excess cornflour. Spoon meringue into piping bag fitted with fluted star pipe, pipe small meringues, about 2.5cm (1in.) in diameter, on to trays, about 2.5cm (1in.) apart.

STEP 2

Pipe as many small meringues as desired, allowing four to six per person. (You can use remaining meringue mixture to pipe larger meringues for future use; these can be stored in airtight container.) Bake meringues in very slow oven — allow 30 minutes for small meringues, 1 hour for larger meringues. Meringues should feel dry and crisp to touch when cooked. Allow to cool on trays.

Make **Coffee Cream** while meringues are cooking: beat butter until creamy, add sugar, beat until combined. Dissolve coffee in hot water, add coffee liqueur, add liquid to creamed mixture, beat until smooth. Join meringues with Coffee Cream. □

Cream of Oyster Soup
Steak with Green Peppercorns
Lemon Beans
Green Salad with Mushrooms
Roast Potatoes
Strawberry Flan

This dinner party gives three-fold enjoyment; you'll enjoy preparing it, cooking it and, best of all, eating it — and so will your guests. Each course is light, beautifully flavoured — and the dessert is superb. This menu serves 6

Opposite, clockwise from top: Green Salad with Mushrooms, Roast Potatoes, Steak with Green Peppercorns and Lemon Beans.

CREAM OF OYSTER SOUP
2 bottles oysters (approx 20 oysters)
2 rashers bacon
60g (2oz) butter
⅓ cup plain flour
2½ cups milk
1 cup cream
2 tablespoons brandy
2 tablespoons dry sherry
salt, pepper
chopped parsley
paprika

Drain oysters, reserving liquid. Remove rind from bacon, chop bacon finely; melt 15g (½oz) butter in pan, add bacon, fry until bacon is crisp, remove from pan, drain on absorbent paper. Melt remaining butter in pan, add flour, cook, stirring 1 minute. Remove from heat, gradually stir in milk and reserved oyster liquid. Return to heat, stir until soup boils and thickens. Add cream and oysters, bacon, brandy and sherry, mix well, heat through but do not allow to boil. Add salt and pepper. Serve sprinkled with chopped parsley and paprika. ▷

STEAK WITH GREEN PEPPERCORNS

6 pieces fillet steak
60g (2oz) butter
2 teaspoons oil
1 tablespoon flour
½ cup dry white wine
2 teaspoons dry sherry
½ cup water
1 beef stock cube
½ teaspoon sugar
2 tablespoons canned
green peppercorns
3 tablespoons cream

Trim steaks, if necessary. Pound steaks lightly. Heat butter and oil in pan, add steaks, cook quickly on both sides to seal in juices. Then cook until they are done to taste. Remove steaks, keep warm. Add flour to pan, stir to combine with pan juices. Stir in the wine, sherry, water, crumbled stock cube, sugar and green peppercorns. Stir until sauce boils, reduce heat, simmer 3 minutes, add cream. Pour sauce over steaks.

LEMON BEANS

500g (1lb) green beans
salt
60g (2oz) butter
1 tablespoon lemon juice

String beans, trim ends, leave them whole. Cook in boiling salted water until just tender; drain. Melt butter in pan, add beans, toss to coat beans in butter, add lemon juice.

GREEN SALAD WITH MUSHROOMS

1 lettuce
250g (8oz) mushrooms
⅓ cup bottled french dressing
½ cucumber
4 shallots

Wash lettuce, dry thoroughly; place in plastic bag in refrigerator to crisp. Wipe mushrooms, slice thinly; put in bowl with french dressing, leave 1 hour. Wipe cucumber skin, slice cucumber thinly; chop shallots. At serving time, drain mushrooms, reserving marinade. Tear lettuce into pieces, place in serving bowl; add cucumber, mushrooms and shallots, sprinkle with enough reserved marinade to coat salad. Toss lightly.

STRAWBERRY FLAN

ALMOND CRUST
185g (6oz) blanched almonds
1 cup coconut
¼ cup sugar
60g (2oz) butter
FILLING
1½ teaspoons gelatine
2 teaspoons water
1 cup sour cream
pinch salt
¾ cup icing sugar
1 teaspoon orange juice
1 teaspoon grated orange rind
1 teaspoon vanilla
1 punnet strawberries
300ml carton thickened cream
GLAZE
2 tablespoons strawberry jam
1 tablespoon water

Almond Crust: Chop almonds finely or blend in blender. Stir in coconut and

sugar. Rub butter into mixture. Reserve 3 tablespoons of crumb mixture for topping. Press remaining crumbs on to base and sides of greased 23cm (9in.) flan tin. Bake in moderately hot oven 12 to 15 minutes or until golden brown, cool. Place reserved crumbs into small pan, stir over low heat until golden, approximately 4 minutes.

Filling: Sprinkle gelatine over water, dissolve over hot water, cool. Combine sour cream, salt, ½ cup sifted icing sugar, orange juice and rind, vanilla and dissolved gelatine. Pour into flan shell. Wash, hull and halve strawberries, arrange over filling. Lightly whip cream and remaining sifted icing sugar. Spoon or pipe around edge of pie. Brush glaze over strawberries. Sprinkle with the toasted crumbs. Refrigerate before serving.

Glaze: Put jam and water in saucepan, stand over low heat 1 minute, push through strainer.

Here's the way to cook beautifully crisp, golden roast potatoes. They cook in a moderate oven, rather than the higher temperature usually needed for roast potatoes, so, if you are cooking a joint, they can cook comfortably in the oven at the same time. After cooking the potatoes, the vegetable shortening can be refrigerated and used again.

1kg (2lb) old potatoes
250g (8oz) solid white
** vegetable shortening**

STEP 1

Peel potatoes, wash well, cut in half lengthways. Place in saucepan of salted water, bring to boil, cover, boil 10 minutes; drain.

STEP 2

Place potatoes on absorbent paper to dry, run a fork over top of potatoes to roughen up surface; this helps the potatoes to crisp well.

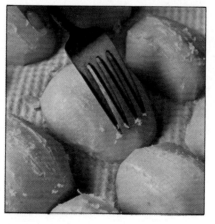

STEP 3

Put chopped vegetable shortening in shallow pan, place in moderate oven 10 minutes or until vegetable shortening has melted. Remove from oven, add potatoes.

STEP 4

Bake in moderate oven 1½ hours or until potatoes are golden brown. After 45 minutes of cooking, drain off half vegetable shortening. Turn potatoes occasionally during cooking. ☐

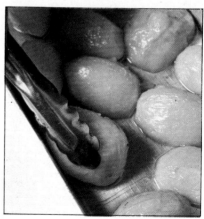

Zucchini and Leek Soup
Tarragon Chicken in Phylo
Creamed Spinach, Mashed Potatoes
Artichoke Salad
Profiteroles with Brandy Alexander Sauce

This menu for 6 starts with a light vegetable soup. There are tender chicken breasts wrapped in phylo for the main course, with accompaniments of creamed spinach, mashed potato and a crisp salad. And, for dessert, little puffs filled with cream and topped with a delicious sauce. The puffs can be prepared some days ahead and deep-frozen. For serving, let them thaw at room temperature, then put them on an oven tray and put into a moderate oven for three to five minutes to re-crisp. Cool, before filling with whipped cream

Opposite, top: Artichoke Salad; below: Tarragon Chicken in Phylo with Creamed Spinach and Mashed Potatoes.

ZUCCHINI AND LEEK SOUP
2 leeks
2 sticks celery
750g (1½lb) zucchini
1 carrot
1 large potato
60g (2oz) butter
3½ cups water
3 chicken stock cubes
salt, pepper
2 tablespoons chopped parsley
⅓ cup cream

Trim leeks, wash thoroughly. Slice celery, leeks and zucchini; peel and slice carrot and potato. Heat butter in large saucepan, add vegetables, stir to coat vegetables in butter. Cover pan, cook over medium heat 5 minutes, stirring occasionally. Do not allow vegetables to brown. Add water, crumbled stock cubes, salt and pepper; mix well. Bring soup to boil, reduce heat, simmer covered 15 minutes or until vegetables are tender. Stir in parsley. Puree vegetables and liquid in electric blender; blend just one cup of soup at a time on medium speed. Return soup to saucepan, add cream, reheat without boiling.

TARRAGON CHICKEN IN PHYLO
90g (3oz) butter
2 teaspoons tarragon
1 tablespoon chopped parsley
1 teaspoon french mustard
3 whole chicken breasts
flour
salt, pepper
30g (1oz) butter, extra
1 tablespoon oil
200g packet phylo pastry
oil for brushing, extra

Combine softened butter, tarragon, parsley and mustard; mix well. Remove skin from chicken breasts. Carefully remove chicken meat from bones, giving six individual pieces. Dust chicken with flour seasoned with salt and pepper. Heat extra butter and the oil in large frying pan, add chicken, cook until golden brown on both sides. Remove from pan, allow to become completely cold.

Use two sheets of phylo pastry for each piece of chicken. Brush first sheet of pastry lightly with extra oil, cover with second sheet of pastry, brush again with oil. Fold pastry in half crossways, brush with oil. Place chicken in centre at one end of pastry. Spread top of chicken with some of the tarragon butter, fold sides of pastry over chicken, roll up to completely enclose chicken. Repeat with remaining chicken, butter and pastry. Place on greased oven tray, brush tops of rolls with oil. Bake in moderately hot oven 10 minutes, reduce heat to moderate, continue to bake further 15 to 20 minutes until golden brown.

Note: If chicken breasts are small, you may need to allow two of the phylo "parcels" per serving, instead of the one we have allowed here. In this case, simply double the recipe.   ▷

CREAMED SPINACH

90g (3oz) butter
2 onions
2 cloves garlic
2 x 250g packets frozen
   chopped spinach
salt, pepper
pinch nutmeg
½ cup cream
6 shallots

Heat butter in pan, add peeled and chopped onions and crushed garlic, cook until onions are tender. Add thawed spinach, salt, pepper and nutmeg; stir until spinach is heated through. Add cream and chopped shallots; cook further 3 minutes.

ARTICHOKE SALAD

1 lettuce
125g (4oz) stuffed olives
½ cup french dressing
400g can artichoke hearts

Wash lettuce, tear into pieces; add stuffed olives and french dressing; toss well. Put into bowl. Arrange drained, rinsed artichokes on top.

PROFITEROLES WITH BRANDY ALEXANDER SAUCE

1 cup water
75g (2½oz) butter
1 cup plain flour
4 eggs
300ml carton thickened cream
BRANDY ALEXANDER SAUCE
125g (4oz) dark chocolate
1 egg yolk
¼ cup water
2 tablespoons Creme de Cacao
1 tablespoon brandy
1 tablespoon cornflour
½ cup milk
½ cup thickened cream

Profiteroles: Place water and butter in pan, bring to boil, add sifted flour all at once. Stir vigorously with wooden spoon over heat until mixture is thick and leaves sides of pan to form a smooth ball; remove from heat; cool. Put cooled paste into small bowl of electric mixer; add eggs, one at a time, beating well after each addition. Spoon teaspoonfuls of mixture on to greased oven trays; bake in hot oven 10 minutes, reduce heat to moderate, bake a further 15 to 20 minutes until golden and crisp. Remove from oven, make a small slit in side of puffs to allow steam to escape; return to oven a few minutes to dry out. When cold, cut puffs in half horizontally. Whip cream until firm peaks form. Place a heaped teaspoonful of cream into bottom of each puff, place remaining half of puff on top. Drizzle Brandy Alexander Sauce over top of each puff. Makes around 30 puffs.

Brandy Alexander Sauce: Put chopped chocolate, egg yolk and water in top of double saucepan. Stir over simmering water until chocolate has melted and mixture thickens slightly. Remove from heat, add Creme de Cacao and brandy; allow to cool. Mix cornflour to a smooth paste with the milk, add to chocolate mixture, stir until smooth. Stir over medium heat until sauce boils and thickens, reduce heat, simmer 2 minutes. Add cream, reheat without boiling.

When guests arrive, it is good to be able to offer them some light, savoury nibble with the before-dinner drink. These little cheese squares are just the thing. The recipe comes from the famous Gaddi's Restaurant in the Peninsula Hotel, Hong Kong. Quantities given make 48.

75g (2½oz) gruyere cheese
75g (2½oz) emmenthaler cheese
1 egg
2½ tablespoons milk
1 clove garlic
⅓ cup plain flour
1 teaspoon baking powder
salt, pepper
12 slices square white bread
oil for deep-frying

STEP 1

Grate cheeses, put into small bowl of electric mixer. Add egg, milk, crushed garlic, sifted flour and baking powder, salt and pepper. Beat on medium speed 5 minutes.

STEP 2

Remove crusts from bread. Spread about 2 tablespoons of mixture on to each slice of bread, right to outer edges. Cut each slice into four squares. (If bread is fresh, remove crusts after you have spread the cheese mixture; the crusts hold the bread firm.)

STEP 3

Put in hot oil, cheese-side down; fry until golden brown on both sides, about 2 minutes, turning once. Drain on absorbent paper. □

A Champagne Breakfast:
Hot Pate Puffs
Chicken and Chablis Quiche
Tomatoes with Guacamole
Eggs with Caviar
Eggs Benedict
Arnold Bennett Omelet
Fruit in Ice

A champagne breakfast — or brunch (combination of breakfast and lunch) — is a happy and easy way to entertain any number of people. Choose a menu from the suggestions given here. Recipes are for 12 but you can easily serve more people by increasing quantities or adding more dishes. The party can begin any time, but around 10.30 to 11am seems popular

Opposite, clockwise from top: Muffins and Croissants, Tomatoes with Guacamole, Eggs with Caviar, Hot Pate Puffs, and Chicken and Chablis Quiche.

THE WINES

Champagne, of course; there's something about the bubbling quality of champagne that makes the party a guaranteed success. You can serve it plain, or with orange juice, or with a dash of green ginger wine. Champagne with orange juice and a dash of Grand Marnier or Cointreau is also delicious.

Or you could serve Champagne Cocktails. To make these, put about half a teaspoon of sugar or half a sugar cube into each glass, add a few drops of Angostura Bitters to colour a delicate pink; fill with ice-cold champagne. A thin slice of orange and/or a dash of brandy can also be added.

Black Velvet — equal quantities of champagne and stout, served in a tall glass — is a popular drink with men.

Or you could serve the fashionable Bellini Cocktail from Rome. Peel one ripe peach, remove stone. Put into blender with ½ teaspoon sugar and two ice cubes, blend until pureed. This is enough for two cocktails. Divide into two glasses, gradually top with well-chilled champagne; agitate with a fork or stirrer until a white froth appears at the top of the drink. Serve immediately. (A dash of Grand Marnier or Cointreau is a delightful addition.)

THE FOOD

You could have a toaster on the table so that guests could cook their own hot toast, crumpets or split muffins. An electric frypan is also a good idea; guests can cook their own bacon and eggs. (Guests do like to help at a party!) Scrambled eggs are also popular; to make them special, mix in some chopped smoked salmon and a little chopped parsley at the last moment.

Croissants are also a favourite; you can buy them beforehand and reheat them in a moderately hot oven for about 10 minutes. Serve with two or three unusual jams — we chose black cherry and marmalade with almonds; add a jar of honey — perhaps containing the honeycomb.

The tiny sausages known as chipolatas also make a good breakfast dish; you could accompany these with bottled mustard sauce. And if you want to make it an English breakfast, add grilled kidneys to the menu.

HOT PATE PUFFS
500g packet puff pastry
1 small onion
375g (12oz) Latvian liverwurst
45g (1½oz) butter
2 tablespoons chopped parsley
½ teaspoon thyme
2 tablespoons cream
1 tablespoon brandy
1 egg yolk
1 tablespoon milk

Cut pastry in half, roll each half out thinly, cut into rounds with 8cm (3in.) cutter. Chop onion. Beat together liverwurst and butter until smooth, add remaining ingredients, except egg yolk and milk, beat again. Spoon teaspoonfuls of pate mixture into centre of each pastry round, brush edges of pastry with combined beaten egg yolk and milk. Fold pastry rounds in half, pinch edges together well. Put on greased oven trays, brush with the remaining egg-yolk mixture, bake in hot oven 10 minutes until golden brown. Makes about 30. ▷

CHICKEN AND CHABLIS QUICHE

PASTRY

1½ cups plain flour
pinch salt
125g (4oz) butter
1 egg yolk
3 tablespoons water

FILLING

1 cooked chicken,
    barbecued or roasted
8 shallots
8 eggs
3 x 300ml cartons cream
¾ cup chablis (or other
    dry white wine)
1 tablespoon french mustard
salt, pepper
paprika
125g (4oz) cheddar cheese

Sift flour and salt into bowl, rub in butter until mixture resembles coarse breadcrumbs. Add combined beaten egg yolk and water, mix to a firm dough, refrigerate 30 minutes. Roll dough out on well-floured board to fit base and sides of 34cm x 26cm (13½in. x 10½in.) baking dish.

Remove chicken meat from the bones, remove skin, chop meat finely, sprinkle over the pastry.

Chop the shallots finely then sprinkle over chicken. Combine in bowl eggs, cream, chablis, mustard, salt and pepper, beat until well combined. Pour over chicken, sprinkle with paprika and grated cheese. Bake in moderate oven 45 to 50 minutes or until set and lightly browned on top. Remove from oven and then cut into slices to serve.

TOMATOES WITH GUACAMOLE

1 avocado
1 clove garlic
1 tablespoon oil
2 teaspoons lemon juice
2 teaspoons grated onion
½ teaspoon chilli powder
2 tablespoons sour cream
salt, pepper
12 small tomatoes

Peel avocado, remove seed, chop roughly, place in blender. Add crushed garlic, oil, lemon juice, onion and chilli powder. Blend on high speed 1 minute or until mixture is smooth. Pour mixture into bowl, stir in sour cream, season with salt and pepper. Refrigerate until ready to use. Cut tops off tomatoes, place a teaspoon of avocado mixture on each.

Note: If desired, two rashers of crisp, crumbled bacon can be added to the avocado mixture.

EGGS WITH CAVIAR

12 hard-boiled eggs
⅓ cup mayonnaise
salt, pepper
60g (2oz) jar caviar

Cut eggs in half, scoop out yolks of each into bowl. Mash together egg yolks and mayonnaise, season with salt and pepper. Place a heaped teaspoonful of egg yolk mixture back into egg halves. Put a small teaspoonful of caviar over egg yolk mixture. If desired, red and black caviar can be used for colour contrast.

EGGS BENEDICT

6 packaged muffins
60g (2oz) butter
12 slices ham
12 eggs
salt, pepper

EASY HOLLANDAISE SAUCE

½ cup cream
½ cup mayonnaise

Split muffins in half, toast each half, keep warm. Heat butter in pan, add ham, cook until light golden brown. Place a slice of ham on each muffin half. Lightly poach eggs, place on ham, top with 1 tablespoon of the Easy Hollandaise Sauce. Season with salt and pepper.

Easy Hollandaise Sauce: Whip ½ cup cream until soft peaks form, place in top of double saucepan with ½ cup mayonnaise over gently simmering water. Stir lightly until sauce is heated through.

ARNOLD BENNETT OMELET

500g (1lb) smoked haddock
90g (3oz) butter
1⅔ cups cream
10 eggs, separated
salt, pepper
2 tablespoons chopped parsley
⅔ cup grated parmesan cheese
¼ cup grated parmesan
    cheese, extra

Put fish in shallow pan, add cold water to cover. Bring to boil, reduce heat, simmer 10 minutes or until fish is tender, drain and cool. Remove any skin and bones from fish, then flake. Melt 30g (1oz) butter in pan, add ⅓ cup of the cream, stir in flaked fish, cook 1 minute; remove from heat. Beat egg yolks with remaining cream, add salt, pepper, parsley, parmesan cheese and fish mixture; mix well. Beat egg whites until soft peaks form, fold into egg-yolk mixture, mix well. Heat remaining butter in large baking dish; when butter is foaming, pour in omelet mixture. Cook over moderate heat until bottom of omelet is golden brown. Sprinkle extra cheese over omelet, place in hot oven 3 to 5 minutes until omelet is cooked.

FRUIT IN ICE

Choose a big bowl; a transparent plastic punch bowl is ideal. Fill it with a selection of fruits in season — ripe peaches, big purple plums, apricots, grapes, cherries. Add a couple of trays of ice-cubes to the bowl. By the time the fruit is ready to be eaten, it will be delightfully chilled.

FROZEN GRAPES

These are an unusual accompaniment to coffee. Simply put bunches of grapes into a plastic bag, put into the freezer until frozen. Eat them while frozen — they have the cool freshness of a sorbet. You can freeze large bunches of grapes and arrange them decoratively in a basket or on a serving plate for guests to help themselves, or you can freeze small bunches for individual servings. □

Antipasto
Spaghetti with Three Sauces
Artichoke Salad
Herbed Garlic Bread
Toasted Nut Cassata

This Italian dinner party for 8 people means easy and informal entertaining (and it is simple enough to halve quantities for 4). There's a taste-tempting antipasto to start, spaghetti with a choice of three quite different sauces, a crisp salad, and superb cassata to complete the meal

Opposite, clockwise from left: Artichoke Salad, Spaghetti, Herbed Garlic Bread, Bolognese Sauce, Antipasto, Tomato and Calamari Sauce, and Spinach Sauce (centre).

ANTIPASTO
1 honeydew melon
1 rockmelon
1 small bunch celery
lettuce leaves
375g (12oz) salami
500g (1lb) pickled mixed vegetables
250g (8oz) black olives
500g (1lb) fresh dates
   (when in season)

Antipasto can be arranged on one large serving plate or individual plates. Cut honeydew and rockmelon in half, remove seeds. Cut honeydew and rockmelon into wedges. Cut celery into 5cm (2in.) lengths. Arrange the lettuce leaves over large plate or individual plates. Arrange melon wedges, sliced salami, mixed vegetables, olives, dates and celery around plate.

Note: Pickled mixed vegetables are available in bulk form at most large delicatessens, or they can be bought in jars from Italian food shops.

SPAGHETTI
750g (1½lb) spaghetti

Cook spaghetti in large boiler or two large saucepans of boiling salted water until tender, approximately 15 minutes. Drain well.

SPINACH SAUCE
2 bunches spinach (about 16 stalks)
2 cloves garlic
60g (2oz) pine nuts
2 teaspoons chopped fresh basil
   (or ½ teaspoon dry basil)
¼ cup chopped parsley
½ cup oil
salt, pepper

Wash spinach; remove white stems; place spinach leaves in saucepan with water that clings to them. Cover; bring to boil. Reduce heat; simmer gently 5 minutes or until spinach is soft. Put spinach in electric blender with crushed garlic, pine nuts, basil and parsley. Blend on medium speed until smooth; gradually add oil in a thin stream. Remove from blender; season with salt and pepper.   ▷

BOLOGNESE SAUCE
1 tablespoon oil
60g (2oz) butter
2 large onions
1kg (2lb) minced steak
1 cup dry red wine
2 x 400g cans whole tomatoes
1 litre (4 cups) water
1 beef stock cube
½ teaspoon basil
½ teaspoon oregano
½ teaspoon thyme
2 tablespoons tomato paste
salt, pepper

Heat oil and butter in large pan, add peeled and sliced onions, cook until onions are transparent. Add meat, mash well. Stir meat until golden brown, pour off all surplus fat. Add wine, undrained mashed tomatoes, water, crumbled stock cube, basil, oregano, thyme and tomato paste. Season with salt and pepper. Stir until sauce boils and thickens, reduce heat, simmer gently uncovered 2 hours or until thick, stirring occasionally.

TOMATO AND CALAMARI SAUCE
500g (1lb) squid
1 tablespoon oil
1 onion
1 clove garlic
1kg (2lb) ripe, firm tomatoes
1 tablespoon tomato paste
2 tablespoons dry white wine
2 teaspoons sugar
salt, pepper
6 shallots
1 tablespoon chopped parsley
2 teaspoons chopped fresh basil
   (or ½ teaspoon dried basil)

Clean squid, cut into 1cm (½in.) squares. Heat oil in large frying pan, add peeled and finely-chopped onion, cook until onion is transparent. Add crushed garlic, cook 1 minute. Add peeled and chopped tomatoes, tomato paste, wine, sugar, salt and pepper; mix well. Bring sauce to boil, add squid, mix well. Reduce heat, simmer uncovered 20 minutes or until squid is tender and sauce has thickened slightly. Stir in chopped shallots, simmer 3 minutes. Stir in the parsley and basil.

Note: Most fish shops or fish counters of large supermarkets sell squid already cleaned, ready for cutting and cooking. In this case, simply cut down the length of the squid, open it out, and cut into squares as directed above. If you can only buy the uncleaned squid, here's how to prepare it for cooking: hold squid firmly with one hand. With the other hand, hold head and pull gently. Head and inside of squid will come away in one compact piece. Remove bone which will be found at open end of squid; it looks like a long, thin piece of plastic. Clean squid under cold running water, then rub off the outer skin. Cut the squid into squares as directed above.

ARTICHOKE SALAD
1 lettuce
2 sticks celery
125g (4oz) stuffed olives
400g can artichoke hearts
2 tablespoons oil
1 tablespoon lemon juice
salt, pepper

Wash lettuce, drain, pat dry, put into plastic bag, refrigerate until crisp. Break into pieces, put in salad bowl, add sliced celery and olives. Drain artichokes, rinse under cold running water, pat dry; cut in half lengthways, add to salad. Just before serving, add oil, lemon juice, salt, pepper; toss well.

HERBED GARLIC BREAD
2 french bread sticks
125g (4oz) butter
2 cloves garlic
2 tablespoons chopped parsley
salt, pepper

Slice bread, cutting just to the bottom of the crust but not right through. Beat butter until light and creamy, fold in crushed garlic, parsley, salt and pepper, mix well. Spread the butter on each side of each slice of bread. Wrap in aluminium foil, bake in moderate oven 15 to 20 minutes.

½ **cup chopped mixed glace fruit**
2 tablespoons brandy
300ml carton cream
2 teaspoons castor sugar
125g (4oz) dark chocolate
15g (½oz) butter
2 litre carton vanilla ice-cream
1 teaspoon vanilla
2 teaspoons cocoa
60g (2oz) slivered almonds
60g (2oz) coconut biscuits
300ml carton cream, extra

Line base of 20cm (8in.) springform pan with aluminium foil. Combine glace fruit and brandy, mix well. Let stand 10 minutes. Whip cream and sugar until thick, fold in fruit and brandy. Spread cream mixture over base of springform pan, freeze. Put chopped chocolate and butter in top of double saucepan, stir over gently-simmering water until melted; cool. Combine half the softened ice-cream and vanilla. Add approximately half a cup of this ice-cream to melted chocolate mixture, mix well. Add chocolate mixture to ice-cream, mix well. The melted chocolate gives the ice-cream a "chocolate chip" texture. Stir in sifted cocoa, mix well. Spread chocolate ice-cream over cream layer; freeze. Spread remaining half-softened ice-cream over chocolate layer. Place almonds in moderate oven 5 minutes or until light golden brown; crush coconut biscuits lightly. Sprinkle combined biscuit crumbs and almonds over top of cassata. Press crumbs and almonds lightly into ice-cream; freeze until firm. Decorate the top with extra whipped cream. □

Chicken and Abalone Soup
Broccoli with Seafood, Steamed Rice
Sweet and Sour Pork
Beef with Green Peppers
Chicken with Black Beans
Many Splendoured Duck
Ginger Wine and Lime Sorbet

Although this Chinese dinner party may seem a lot of work, most of the preparation — cutting of meat and vegetables — can be done the day before and the food packed in plastic bags and refrigerated. With the exception of the duck, the cooking time for each course is short. The sorbet for dessert can be made a day or two ahead. This delicious menu serves 8

Opposite, clockwise from top left: Chicken with Black Beans, Chicken and Abalone Soup, Broccoli with Seafood, Ginger Wine and Lime Sorbet, Beef with Green Peppers, Sweet and Sour Pork.

CHICKEN AND ABALONE SOUP
1 whole chicken breast
440g can abalone
½ x 230g can bamboo shoots
60g (2oz) mushrooms
6 shallots
1 egg
1 teaspoon oil
1½ litres (6 cups) chicken stock
1cm (½in.) piece green ginger
salt, pepper
3 tablespoons cornflour
3 tablespoons water
1 tablespoon dry sherry
2 teaspoons soy sauce
2 egg whites
2 tablespoons water, extra

Remove skin from chicken breast, cut meat from breast bones then cut into thin strips, approximately 8cm x 5mm (3in. x ¼in.). Drain abalone, reserve liquid, slice and cut abalone into thin 5mm (¼in.) strips. Drain bamboo shoots, cut into fine strips. Remove stalks from mushrooms, slice mushrooms thinly; chop shallots. Lightly beat egg; heat oil in pan, add egg, swirl egg in pan to coat base evenly. Loosen edges of egg pancake, turn and cook other side. Remove from pan, roll up, slice into thin strips. Place chicken stock, reserved abalone liquid, grated ginger and abalone in a large saucepan. Bring to boil, add chicken, bamboo shoots, mushrooms, salt and pepper. Bring to boil, reduce heat, simmer uncovered 5 minutes. Remove pan from heat, gradually stir in combined cornflour, water, dry sherry and soy sauce. Return pan to heat, stir until soup boils, reduce heat, simmer uncovered 2 minutes. Stir in shallots and pancake strips. Lightly beat egg whites with extra water, stir into soup in a thin stream.

BROCCOLI WITH SEAFOOD
250g (8oz) broccoli
230g can bamboo shoots
1 small carrot
500g (1lb) green prawns
¼ teaspoon salt
½ egg white
2 teaspoons cornflour
250g (8oz) squid
oil for deep-frying
5mm (¼in.) piece green ginger
SAUCE
½ teaspoon dry sherry
¼ teaspoon sesame oil
¼ cup chicken stock
½ teaspoon salt
½ teaspoon sugar
1 teaspoon cornflour

Cut broccoli into small flowerets, put in saucepan with enough boiling salted water to cover; boil 1 minute, drain, rinse under cold water, drain again. Cut bamboo shoots into thin slices. Peel carrot, cut into thin slices. Parboil bamboo shoots and carrot in boiling salted water 1 minute, drain. Shell and devein prawns; combine salt, egg white and cornflour in bowl, add prawns, mix well. Remove bone and skin from squid, cut down centre. Spread squid out flat with the inside facing upwards. Make shallow knife cuts across squid in diamond shape to tenderise the squid and make them curl attractively when cooked. Cut squid into 2.5cm (1in.) diagonal slices. Heat oil in pan, deep-fry prawns and squid until prawns and squid both curl up, approximately 1 to 2 minutes, remove from pan, drain. Remove excess oil from pan, leaving 1 tablespoon of oil in pan. Heat this oil, add peeled and sliced ginger, fry 1 minute, add broccoli, bamboo shoots and carrot, toss 2 minutes; add prawns, squid and sauce, toss until sauce boils and thickens.

Sauce: Combine all the sauce ingredients, mix well. ▷

SWEET AND SOUR PORK
1 tablespoon soy sauce
1 egg yolk
1 tablespoon cornflour
500g (1lb) lean pork chops
1 red pepper
1 green pepper
3 canned pineapple rings
½ cup cornflour, extra
oil for deep-frying
2 cloves garlic
SAUCE
3 tablespoons white vinegar
3 tablespoons sugar
3 tablespoons water
3 tablespoons tomato sauce
½ teaspoon salt
1½ teaspoons cornflour

Combine soy sauce, egg yolk and cornflour in bowl, stir well. Remove rind from chops, cut chops into 2.5cm (1in.) cubes, place into soy sauce mixture, stir until meat is coated. Cover, leave 1 hour; stir occasionally. Combine all ingredients for sauce, mix well. Seed red and green peppers, cut into 2.5cm (1in.) slices, cut pineapple rings into quarters. Add extra cornflour to pork mixture, mix until pork is well coated. Heat oil in pan, deep-fry pork until golden brown and cooked through, about 7 minutes; drain well. Pour off excess oil, leaving 1 tablespoon oil in pan. Add crushed garlic, cook 1 minute, remove from pan. Add red and green peppers and pineapple quarters to pan, cook quickly, stirring constantly for 3 minutes, add pork and sauce, stir until sauce boils and thickens.

BEEF WITH GREEN PEPPERS
375g (12oz) fillet steak in one piece
1 tablespoon soy sauce
1 tablespoon water
2 teaspoons dry sherry
3 teaspoons cornflour
2 green peppers
3 tablespoons oil
2 cloves garlic

Remove fat and sinew from meat. Cut meat into 5mm (¼in.) slices then into 5mm (¼in.) thin strips. Combine soy sauce, water, dry sherry and cornflour in bowl, add meat, mix well. Stand 30 minutes. Seed peppers, cut into 5mm (¼in.) strips. Heat 1 tablespoon oil in pan, add peppers, toss gently 2 minutes, remove from pan. Add remaining 2 tablespoons oil to pan, add crushed garlic, cook 1 minute; add beef, and toss and cook quickly until meat is golden brown. Add peppers to meat in pan, toss until well mixed.

CHICKEN WITH BLACK BEANS
2 whole chicken breasts
1 tablespoon soy sauce
1 teaspoon sugar
½ teaspoon salt
2 teaspoons cornflour
1 teaspoon dry sherry
1cm (½in.) piece green ginger
1 red pepper
2 onions
4 shallots
1 tablespoon black beans
4 cloves garlic
4 tablespoons oil

Remove chicken breasts from bones, giving four individual pieces. Cut each piece in half lengthwise, then cut each half into four pieces. Combine meat with soy sauce, sugar, salt, cornflour, dry sherry and grated green ginger; mix well; stand 1 hour. Seed pepper, cut into 1cm (½in.) cubes; peel onions, cut into 1cm (½in.) cubes, cut shallots into 2.5cm (1in.) lengths. Finely chop black beans with garlic. Heat 1 tablespoon oil in pan, add onions, cook 2 minutes; add pepper, cook further 1 minute; remove from pan. Heat remaining 3 tablespoons oil in pan, add black bean mixture, cook 1 minute; add chicken, cook, stirring, 5 minutes or until cooked through. Stir in shallots, onions and pepper, mix well.

GINGER WINE AND LIME SORBET
2 cups water
½ cup ginger wine
2 tablespoons lime juice
1 cup sugar
⅓ cup water, extra
2 egg whites

Combine water, ginger wine and lime juice. Pour into deep 20cm cake tin, freeze until firm. Place sugar and extra water in pan. Stir over low heat until sugar is dissolved, bring to boil, boil rapidly for 4 minutes, remove from heat. Beat egg whites until soft peaks form, pour the hot syrup into the egg whites in a very slow thin stream, beating on high speed all the time. Beat in frozen ginger wine mixture. Freeze until firm, beat mixture until smooth, refreeze. To serve, put fruit salad into eight serving glasses, flake sorbet with fork and pile on top of fruit salad.

Note: Any colourful combination of fruit can be used for the fruit salad.

There may seem a lot of garlic and ginger in this recipe — and there is! — but it merely flavours the cooking liquid and is then discarded. And the flavour is superb!

125g (4oz) green ginger
1 knob garlic
1.5kg (3lb) duck
2 cups water
½ cup soy sauce
⅓ cup honey

STEP 1
Scrape ginger; with the side of meat mallet or rolling pin, pound ginger lightly then cut into 1cm (½in.) cubes. Pound garlic with cleaver or mallet, remove skin.

STEP 2
Place duck, ginger, garlic and water in a large saucepan, bring to boil. Add soy sauce, bring to boil, reduce heat, simmer gently covered 2 hours, turn duck once after 1¼ hours.

STEP 3
Remove duck from pan, allow to cool slightly. Strain and reserve liquid, discard ginger and garlic.

STEP 4
Return liquid and duck to pan; bring to boil. Add honey, reduce heat, simmer uncovered 30 minutes, basting frequently.

STEP 5
Remove duck from pan, cool. Cut duck into pieces, Chinese-style, as shown. The wings are cut into three; the leg and thigh into three pieces, at joints; separate breast from back by cutting through rib bones; cut breast down centre, then cut each breast across into four — this will give you 8 pieces; cut across back piece to give 5 pieces. Arrange back pieces down centre of serving plate, pile breast pieces on top, then wings and leg and thigh pieces on both sides. Bring sauce back to boil, pour over duck.

Duck can be cooked in advance, chopped as above, then gently reheated in the sauce. □

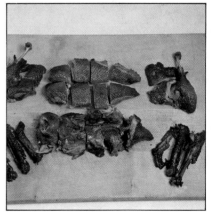

Prawns Kiev
Smorgasbord Platter
French Mustard Potato Salad
Spinach Coleslaw
Fruit and Cheese Platter
Plum Sorbet

Full of pleasant surprises, this dinner party menu for 8 would be tempting even in the hottest weather. Entree is Prawns Kiev — prawns stuffed with a herbed garlic butter. The main course offers a delightful variety of good things — tender beef, served with a horseradish cream, and smorgasbord accompaniment, with salads. Finale to the meal is a cheese and fruit platter served with a light plum sorbet

Opposite, clockwise from front: Smorgasbord Platter, Fruit and Cheese Platter, Spinach Coleslaw, French Mustard Potato Salad, and Prawns Kiev.

SMORGASBORD PLATTER
4 hard-boiled eggs
454g bottle or can baby whole or sliced beetroot
1 cabanossi (or cabana) sausage
125g (4oz) mixed pickles
3 tomatoes
1 small cucumber
400g can artichoke hearts
225g can baby whole corn
1 lettuce
125g (4oz) black olives
125g (4oz) stuffed olives
60g (2oz) salami
60g (2oz) sliced ham deluxe (or ham)
8 small roll-mops

Shell eggs, cut in half. Drain beetroot. Slice cabanossi diagonally. Drain pickles. Thinly slice cucumber and tomatoes. Drain artichokes. Drain corn. Place crisp lettuce leaves around edge of large serving platter or several plates. Arrange eggs, beetroot, tomatoes, black olives, stuffed olives, sliced salami, ham, cabanossi, pickles, cucumber, artichokes, corn and prepared Spicy Chicken Legs, Roast Beef and roll-mops decoratively over plate. Cover and refrigerate until ready to serve.

ROAST BEEF
2.5kg (5lb) piece whole rump
salt, pepper
60g (2oz) butter

Put meat into baking dish, rub meat all over with salt and pepper. Add butter. Bake in hot oven for 30 minutes, reduce heat to moderate for 30 minutes, increase heat to hot again, bake further 30 minutes. Allow meat to cool in pan, then place meat on plate, cover and refrigerate until ready to serve. Cut into thin slices. Serve Horseradish Cream (see over) as an accompaniment.

Note: The whole rump is an economical buy, generally available at special prices from butchers. There is practically no waste, the meat cuts well and you and your guests will find it beautifully tender. ▷

122

HORSERADISH CREAM

½ cup sour cream
4 tablespoons bottled
   horseradish relish
1 teaspoon sugar
2 tablespoons chopped parsley
salt, pepper

Combine all ingredients in a bowl, mix well until combined.

SPICY CHICKEN LEGS

8 large chicken legs
1 egg
½ cup flour
2 teaspoons curry powder
¼ teaspoon cinnamon
1 teaspoon dry mustard
salt, pepper
1 teaspoon paprika
oil for deep-frying

Coat chicken legs with beaten egg, then roll in combined dry ingredients. Place four chicken legs into deep hot oil, fry for 5 minutes or until chicken legs are golden brown and cooked through; drain on absorbent paper. Do not have oil too hot or chicken will brown too quickly and not cook through. Repeat with remaining chicken legs. Place chicken legs on to baking tray, cover and refrigerate until ready to serve. Serve the chicken legs cold or reheat in a moderate oven, uncovered, for 10 minutes or until heated through.

FRENCH MUSTARD POTATO SALAD

1kg (2lb) potatoes
1 red pepper
½ cup bottled french dressing
2 teaspoons french mustard
2 tablespoons chopped chives
salt, pepper

Peel potatoes, cut into 2.5cm (1in.) cubes, cook in boiling salted water until just tender, drain immediately. Seed pepper, chop into small pieces, combine with potatoes. Combine in screw-top jar french dressing, mustard, chives, salt and pepper, shake to combine well. Just before serving, add to potato salad and toss well.

SPINACH COLESLAW

¼ cabbage
1 small bunch spinach
2 medium onions
1 small red pepper
1 small green pepper
2 medium carrots
salt, pepper
1 teaspoon sugar
½ cup bottled french dressing

Wash cabbage and spinach, shake off excess water. Finely shred cabbage and spinach. Peel onions, cut in half, then slice finely. Finely slice seeded red and green peppers, scrape and finely slice carrots. Place all prepared vegetables into large bowl; toss well. Refrigerate until ready to serve. Add combined salt, pepper, sugar and french dressing; toss well. Spoon into serving bowl.

FRUIT AND CHEESE PLATTER

Choose any of the fresh fruits in season, and perhaps three favourite varieties of cheese.

For the platter shown we used papaw, rockmelon, mango, pears, strawberries and dates. The cheeses used were 250g (8oz) derby sage, 250g (8oz) roquefort and 250g (8oz) smoked cheese with chives. Serve with the Plum Sorbet.

PLUM SORBET

825g can dark plums
¾ cup water
½ cup sugar
2 tablespoons lemon juice
3 egg whites
⅓ cup sugar, extra

Drain plums, reserve syrup. Remove seeds from plums. Put roughly-chopped plums and syrup into blender, blend until smooth, or beat well until smooth. Push plum mixture through sieve. Put sieved plum puree, water, sugar and lemon juice into saucepan, stir over low heat until sugar has dissolved. Bring to boil, remove from heat immediately, allow to become cold. Pour into deep 20cm (8in.) cake tin. Freeze until partially set. Beat egg whites until soft peaks form, gradually add extra sugar, beat until sugar has dissolved. Using fork, fold meringue through plum mixture. Return to freezer, freeze until firm, stirring occasionally with fork.

125g (4oz) butter
2 tablespoons chopped parsley
2 teaspoons french mustard
1 clove garlic
salt, pepper
1kg (2lb) large green king prawns
flour
2 eggs
⅓ cup milk
packaged dry breadcrumbs
oil for deep-frying

STEP 1

Put butter in bowl, beat until soft; add parsley, mustard, crushed garlic, salt and pepper; mix well. Put butter mixture on to greaseproof paper, form into a thin roll. Refrigerate until butter is hard. Cut butter into 2cm (¾in.) slices. Remove shells and veins from prawns. Take two prawns for each butter slice and pound two prawns together into a flat circle.

STEP 2

With wet hands mould prawns around butter. Repeat with remaining prawns and butter.

STEP 3

Roll prawns lightly in flour, dip into combined beaten eggs and milk, then roll in breadcrumbs. Repeat egg-and-breadcrumb process to give firm coating. Prawns can then be refrigerated until serving time.

STEP 4

Just before serving, deep-fry in hot oil for approximately 3 minutes or until prawns are cooked. □

Index

Cup and Spoon Measurements

To ensure accuracy in your recipes use the standard metric measuring equipment approved by Standards Australia:

(a) 250 millilitre cup for measuring liquids. A litre jug *(capacity 4 cups)* is also available.

(b) a graduated set of four cups – measuring 1 cup, half, third and quarter cup – for items such as flour, sugar, etc. When measuring in these fractional cups, level off at the brim.

(c) a graduated set of four spoons: tablespoon *(20 millilitre liquid capacity)*, teaspoon *(5 millilitre)*, half and quarter teaspoons. The Australian, British and American teaspoon each has 5ml capacity.

Approximate cup and spoon conversion chart

Australian	American & British
1 cup	1¼ cups
¾ cup	1 cup
⅔ cup	¾ cup
½ cup	⅔ cup
⅓ cup	½ cup
¼ cup	⅓ cup
2 tablespoons	¼ cup
1 tablespoon	4 teaspoons

Oven Temperatures

Electric	C°	F°
Very slow	120	250
Slow	150	300
Moderately slow	160-180	325-350
Moderate	180-200	375-400
Moderately hot	210-230	425-450
Hot	240-250	475-500
Very hot	260	525-550

Gas	C°	F°
Very slow	120	250
Slow	150	300
Moderately slow	160	325
Moderate	180	350
Moderately hot	190	375
Hot	200	400
Very hot	230	450

We have used large eggs with an average weight of 60g each in all recipes.
ALL SPOON MEASUREMENTS ARE LEVEL.
Note: NZ, Canada, USA *and* UK *all use 15ml tablespoons.*